DESIGN YOUR
NATURAL MIDWEST GARDEN

PATRICIA HILL

TRAILS BOOKS
Madison, Wisconsin

Library of Congress Control Number: 200792083
ISBN 13: 978-1-931599-81-8
ISBN 10: 1-931599-81-5
Editor: Mark Knickelbine
Designer: Kathie Campbell
Cover Photo: ©Darryl R. Beers, Shooting Star

Printed in China by C&C Offset Printing Co.
12 11 10 09 08 07   6 5 4 3 2 1

TRAILS BOOKS, a division of Big Earth Publishing
923 Williamson Street • Madison, WI 53703
(800) 258-5830 • www.trailsbooks.com

DESIGN YOUR
NATURAL MIDWEST GARDEN

PATRICIA HILL

TRAILS BOOKS
Madison, Wisconsin

Contents

Preface

I HAVE WRITTEN THIS BOOK for those who live on a lot in a typical town or suburb and want to make their grounds sustainable, more characteristically Midwestern, more enjoyable, and, not incidentally, more economical and easier to maintain.

I have personally grown or studied all of the plants described in this book, but I have relied heavily on two sources: Floyd Swink and Gerould Wilhelm's *Plants of the Chicago Region*, 1994, which provides information on plant communities, and on Dick Young's *Kane County: Wild Plants and Natural Areas*, offering descriptions of plants and information on plant size. My undying gratitude is extended to these scientists. Without the excellent guidance of their books, my own book could not have been written, nor could my garden even have been planned or planted. I am also fortunate to have participated in many field trips led by these three authors that have been invaluable to me.

I've lived in three homes over the past 35 or so years—a ranch house on a 3/4 acre lot in an oak savanna with a tiny creek at the back, a townhouse in a beautiful natural area adjacent to a forest preserve, and, most recently, in a 1927 Sears bungalow on a small lot (only 50' x 125') in an older, traditional neighborhood. Each home site provided unique opportunities for creating gardens. When I talk about my own gardens in the book, I may be referring to a garden created at any one of these three sites.

I call all of the plants by their common names so as to not daunt those who have never gardened before or have no interest in nomenclature. I attach the Latin name only once when I first describe the plant.

Conservation is getting nowhere because it is incompatible with our Abramic concept of land. We abuse the land because we regard it as a commodity belonging to us. When we see land as a community to which we belong, we may begin to use it with love and respect. There is no other way for land to survive the impact of mechanized man. —Aldo Leopold, *A Sand County Almanac*

When you're driving the sweet empty roads between home and Fargo, endless and empty possibilities surround you. That's the view I like, all nothing particular. Sky, field and the sounds of human attempts to alter same so small and unimportant and forgettable as you whiz by. I like blending into the distance. Passing shelter belts and fields that divide the world into squares, I always think of the chaos underneath. The signs and boundaries and markers on the surface are laid out strict, so recent that they make me remember how little time has passed since everything was high grass, taller than we stand, thicker, with no end. Beasts covered it. Birds by the million. Buffalo. If you sat still in one place they would parade past you for three days, head to head. Goose flocks blotted the sun, their cries like great storms. Bears. No ditches. Sloughs, rivers, and over all the winds, the vast winds blowing and careening with nothing in the way to stop them-no buildings, fence lines to strum, no drive-in movie screens to bang against, not even trees. —Louise Erdrich, *The Bingo Palace*

A person born on the plains, having changed his home to the hills or mountains, longs for the vast open spaces, where the horizon seems to touch the earth and where freedom speaks louder than anywhere else in the world. —Jens Jensen, *Siftings*

We of the Middle West are living on the prairie. The prairie has a beauty of its own and we should recognize and accentuate this natural beauty, its quiet level. —Frank Lloyd Wright

Introduction

WHY NATIVE PLANTS?

THE MIDWESTERN CLIMATE IS HARSH—it has cold winters with chilling winds and temperatures that may drop to 20°. below zero, coupled with hot summers with high humidity and sometimes long droughts. Most gardening books seem to have been written by people who live in Connecticut, in hardiness zones 6 or 7, with warmer winters, cooler summers, more rainfall, and ericaceous soils that enable lush growth of rhododendrons, azaleas, and other broadleaf evergreens, none of which grow well in the Midwest. In addition, national gardening magazines almost never depict Midwestern gardens, making these publications virtually useless to us as horticultural guides.

Unlike inhabitants of other regions of the country, Midwesterners do not have an intact native landscape to emulate. The northeastern part of our country has its forests, Florida has its tropical vegetation, the southwest has its deserts, the Great Plains have their shortgrass prairie, and the northwest has its rainforests. Although home and corporate landscapes throughout the country have been homogenized so that Phoenix looks like Philadelphia, which looks like Minneapolis, most of the undeveloped countryside is unique to its region. In the Midwest, however, the tallgrass prairie is gone. With the invention of the steel plow in 1835, the prairie was broken up within a period of 50 years-barely 1/10 of 1 percent of the original prairie remains. Some small remnant of our heritage is found along railroad tracks and sometimes in old cemeteries, where prairie flowers and grasses still grow, usually mixed in with Eurasian weeds. This leads us to assume our native plants are weeds, as well.

Our people have become disconnected from the idea of a past and a tomorrow, and are wholly oblivious to the distinction between a field of weeds and a land with the vital power to evolve and renew itself. —Gerould Wilhelm, Coffee Creek Center Web Site

But in the last few years, the beauty of the Midwestern indigenous landscape has been discovered, and distinct Midwest gardening and landscaping styles are evolving. The "Prairie Spirit" was first advocated and practiced by O. C. Symonds, Jens Jensen, and Walter Burley Griffin. These three "Prairie Landscape Architects" of the early twentieth century have inspired and shaped the prairie and savanna restorations taking place throughout the Midwest today.

The Middle West is just beginning to evolve a new style of architecture, interior decoration, and landscape gardening, in an effort to create the perfect home amid the prairie states. This movement is founded on the fact that one of the greatest assets which any country or natural part of it can have, is a strong national or regional character, especially in the homes of the common people. Its westernism grows out of the most striking peculiarity of middle-western scenery, which is the prairie, i.e., flat or gently rolling land that was treeless when the white man came to Illinois. —Wilhelm Miller, *The Prairie Spirit in Landscape Gardening*

The true father of the Midwest ecology movement is Aldo Leopold, scientist, naturalist, teacher, philosopher, writer, and poet. Born in Burlington, Iowa, he earned a master's degree in forestry from Yale University; upon graduation, in 1909, he joined the Forestry Service. In 1924, he was assigned to the U.S. Forest Products Laboratory at Madison, Wisconsin, and began teaching at the University of Wisconsin in 1928. It was during this period that he developed his land ethic.

The land ethic simply enlarges the boundaries of the community to include soils, waters, plants, and animals, or collectively: the land.
In short, a land ethic changes the role of Homo sapiens from conqueror of the land community to plain member and citizen of it. It implies respect for his fellow-members, and also respect for the community as such. —Aldo Leopold, *A Sand County Almanac*

In 1934, Leopold suggested that the newly purchased land for an arboretum at the university could provide "a sample of what Dane County looked like when our ancestors arrived here." From 1936 to 1940, Leopold and William Longnecker, campus landscape architect and executive director of the arboretum, oversaw the effort to reestablish a tallgrass prairie, the first-ever effort to restore a native ecosystem on disturbed land. Two hundred recruits from the Civilian Conservation Corps planted seeds, sods, and transplants of 43 different species of prairie grasses and forbs. Curtis Prairie, named after John Curtis, the first ecology professor at the university, still serves as a laboratory for prairie restorations.

That same season, Leopold began restoring the land at his weekend and summer home, an abandoned, derelict farm in Baraboo on the sandy banks of the Wisconsin River, an hour north of Madison. The house had burned down, so a chicken coop, lovingly called "The Shack," was turned into a laboratory and living quarters for himself, and his family, friends, and graduate students. The genesis of his book, *A Sand County Almanac*, took place here. Published posthumously in 1949, it remains one of the finest nature books ever written.

A land ethic, then, reflects the existence of an ecological conscience, and this in turn reflects a conviction of individual responsibility for the health of the land. Health is the capacity of the land for self-renewal. Conservation is our effort to understand and preserve this capacity. —Aldo Leopold, *A Sand County Almanac*

The prairie, in all its expressions, is a massive, subtle place, with a long history of contradiction and misunderstanding. But it is worth the effort at comprehension. It is, after all, at the center of our national identity.
—Wayne Fields, *Lost Horizon*, from *PrairyErth* by William Least Heat-Moon

WHAT IS A PRAIRIE?

PRAIRIE n. an extensive area of flat or rolling grassland esp. the plain of central North America. [Fr.<*Ofr praerie* <Lat. *Pratum, meadow.*] *The American Heritage Dictionary*, Second College Edition

The tallgrass prairie is indigenous to parts of Ohio, Indiana, Michigan, most of Illinois and Missouri, southern Wisconsin, all of Iowa, southern and western Minnesota, and eastern parts of North and South Dakota, Nebraska, Kansas, and Oklahoma. Before settlement of these areas, tallgrass prairie covered 264,000 square miles. But with the invention of the steel plow in 1837 that could easily cut through the heavy sods of the tallgrasses, the prairie disappeared almost entirely in 50 years According to Neil Diboll, owner of Northwind Nursery in Westfield, Wisconsin, Iowa is the most ecologically degraded state in the United States (Illinois comes in second); the economic value of its deep black soil led to the destruction of the prairie that created it.

Iowa has the highest concentration of prime farmland in the world; but... , , , for every bushel of corn that Iowa grows, it loses two bushels of soil. After just a century of farming, its rich prairie soil, which took millennia to make, is half gone. What is left has had the life burned from it by herbicides, pesticides and relentless monocropping. Petrochemicals fuel its zombie productivity.
—Evan Eisenberg, *The Ecology of Eden*

Floyd Swink and Gerould Wilhelm, authors of *Plants of the Chicago Region*, tell us that a prairie consists of grasses and forbs (herbaceous plants other than grasses or sedges) that form a dry, flammable groundcover in autumn; regular autumnal fires ignited by dry lightning or set by Native Americans were an essential part of sustaining the habitat.

It is often remarked, "native plants are coarse." How humiliating to hear an American speak so of plants with which the Great Master has decorated his land! To me no plant is more refined than that which belongs. —Jens Jensen, *Siftings*

Many prairie flowers are common perennials that have been familiar to us for years, not only in the Midwest, but also throughout the United States and Europe. As I look through a nationally distributed garden catalogue, I see a dozen native prairie flowers such as New England Aster, Showy Black-eyed Susan, Purple Coneflower, Blazing Star, Foxglove Beard Tongue, Obedient Plant, Spiderwort, False Sunflower, and Sneezeweed.

But there are so many more not found in general catalogues, with intriguing names such as Prairie Smoke, Lead Plant, Thimbleweed, Queen-of-the-Prairie, Rattlesnake Master, Compass Plant, Prairie Dock, Purple Joe Pye Weed, Side-oats Grama, Purple Love Grass, Indian Grass, Prairie Dropseed, and on and on, a richer and more diverse mix of vascular plants than anywhere else in the country, but they remain virtually unknown.

It would be difficult to circumscribe another area of the North Temperate Zone with such geologic and physiographic diversity-our native flora, consisting of 1638 taxa, reflects this. —Floyd Swink and Gerould Wilhelm, *Plants of the Chicago Region*

To try to force plants to grow in soil or climate unfitted for them and against nature's methods will sooner or later spell ruin. Besides, such a method tends to make the world commonplace and to destroy the ability to unfold an interesting and beautiful landscape out of home environments. Life is made rich and the world beautiful by each section developing its own beauty. —Jens Jensen, *Siftings*

Landscaping with native plants is a new way of landscaping, a new way of gardening that celebrates biodiversity and sustainability.

What is biodiversity? It means the variety of all forms of life on earth. Its complexity depends on genetic, species, and ecosystem variations. Biodiversity helps natural communities survive catastrophes—it is an insurance policy. Our living resources today are threatened by habitat destruction, pollution, global climate changes, and invasion by alien species.

And what is sustainability? Nature, if left alone, regenerates itself: seeds grow into plants, bloom, set seed, and die; the dead material then decays and fertilizes the new seeds. It is an efficient, closed system; its cycles and rhythms form the wheel of life. Sustainability means obeying the rules of endless recycling. Nothing needs to be brought in, such as fertilizers, pesticides, or water; nothing leaves the system either, not even dead leaves or rainwater. Deep prairie roots absorb rain where it falls; leaves decay and become mulch and fertilizer. Sustainability means belonging to the same club to which every other living thing on the earth belongs.

WHY PLANT NATIVE PLANTS?

THERE ARE ENVIRONMENTAL, aesthetic, and spiritual reasons to do so.

➤ Native gardens are sustainable. They are well suited to the climate and soil conditions of the area where they are found naturally—they are grown successfully with little effort. Native plants, once established, don't need babying: no watering, no staking, no pruning, no deadheading, no dividing, no fertilizing, no pesticides or fungicides. Nothing needs to be brought in and nothing needs to be taken away.

➤ Native gardens contribute to the overall quality of the environment by improving air, water, and soil properties. The immense root systems of tallgrasses, in particular, absorb rain, thereby preventing runoff, erosion, and flooding; they enrich the soil with their decaying matter; and they have the ability to sink carbon.

➤ Native landscapes give us the means to reconnect and interact with the natural world around us. Native landscapes provide habitat for birds, butterflies, frogs, toads, and salamanders; and they offer fascinating places for children to play in and explore.

➤ Every native plant is part of a community of plants, animals, insects, and microorganisms that keeps species in check there are no native equivalents of Purple Loosestrife or Garlic Mustard or Buckthorn that destroy natural communities.

➤ Native landscapes celebrate the character, history, and identity of a particular community and region.

Native landscaping is the key to the long-term health of our environment. Native landscaping works with rather than against nature. In native landscapes and gardens the plants do the work for us; in turn, we must be willing to risk losing control. A landscape of native plants is not static—it is dynamic. It is free and alive—it will renew itself. If you have a passion to make a difference in the world, plant native plants in your own little piece of the planet.

Scientists around the world are concerned by what they see as global homogenization of plant life caused by the introduction of non-native plants and the rise of "weedy" organisms supremely adapted to human landscapes—a sort of botanical version of the homogenization of international cuisine caused by the Big Mac.
—Janet Marinelli, *Stalking the Wild Amaranth*

Perhaps the blurring of provincial lines and the need for everyone to identify with the human condition in general will have positive results for the future, but preservation and promotion of local, state, and regional traditions will continue to make life more meaningful.
—Leo E. Olivia, *Kansas: A Hard Land in the Heartland*, from *PrairyErth* by William Least Heat-Moon

One reason Frank Lloyd Wright was for many years regarded as old-fashioned (Phillip Johnson, in his International Style days, famously dismissed Wright as "the greatest architect of the nineteenth century") is that, even as he set about inventing the space of modern architecture, he continued to insist on the importance of Here—of the American ground. Wright always upheld the value of a native and regional architecture (one for the prairie, another for the desert) and resisted universal culture in all its guise—whether it came dressed in the classicism of Thomas Jefferson, the internationalism of the Beaux Arts movement, or the modernism of Le Corbusier.
—Michael Pollen, *A Place of My Own*

For everything there is a season, and a time to every purpose under the heaven.   —Ecclesiastes 3:1

Live in each season as it passes;
breathe the air, drink the drink,
taste the fruit, and resign yourself to
the influences of each.

—Henry David Thoreau

GARDENING AS A WAY OF LIFE

GARDENING IS ABOUT SOWING and reaping. A gardener is in touch with the rhythms of the universe. Prairie Smoke blooms in spring, Black-eyed Susan in summer, asters and goldenrods in autumn. Birds return in spring; green leaves emerge from dead-looking sticks; April showers bring May flowers. The sun is high in the sky and the days are long in summer; fireflies twinkle in July evenings. In August the Big Dipper is low in the sky, and nighthawks flock prior to their southern migration. Fruits and berries ripen and birds fly south in late summer and autumn. The days grow short when you reach September and monarch butterflies begin their exodus to Mexico. Leaves turn to brilliant colors in fall, then drop. It snows in winter. Everything happens in its turn; the inexorable cycle moves at its own pace, never changing.

All sorts of things and weather
Must be taken in together,
To make up a year
And a Sphere.   —Ralph Waldo Emerson

The preferred infrastructural aesthetic demands that the outdoors look ever more like the indoors.
—James M. Patchett and Gerould S. Wilhelm, "Designing Sustainable Systems: Fact or Fancy"

We have, however, lost our sense of the rhythm of the seasons and of life itself.. Our homes and cars and offices are heated in winter and cooled in summer; we shop in climate-controlled indoor malls; our garages are attached to our houses, making it unnecessary to ever set foot in our own outdoors. We eat apples in spring and strawberries in fall. We plant never-changing landscapes-someone, somewhere, seems to have decreed that everyone must install yews next to the house foundation and then prune them into green muffins that look the same twelve months of the year, sometimes embellished with annuals that bloom unchangingly from May until a killing frost.

D. H. Lawrence says, "The rhythm of the cosmos is something we cannot get away from without bitterly impoverishing our lives . . . we are cut off from the great sources of our inward nourishment and renewal, sources which flow eternally in the universe." (D. H. Lawrence, *Marriage and the Living Cosmos*)

At Christmas I no more desire a rose
Than wish a snow in May's new-fangled mirth;
But like of each thing that in season grows.

—William Shakespeare

Gardening has to be more than a hobby, more than beautifying our grounds. It has to be a way of life, connecting us to the rhythm of the cosmos and the natural world from which our automobiles and our air-conditioned, central-heated lives have divorced us. Gardens are a fine art form, but a democratic art that anyone can participate in, regardless of talent, social status, or pocketbook. Gardens have to stir us and ignite our passions.

By creating outdoor spaces for sitting, dining, entertaining, and playing, gardens become extensions of our houses and part of our everyday living. We can make welcoming entrances; create views to enjoy through our windows; attract birds, butterflies, and bees; provide greenways for wildlife; modify the microclimate around our own houses; and improve the quality of life for ourselves and our planet.

You don't have to grow a prairie in order to enjoy prairie plants. Arrange them in open borders or in an island bed, or use them to replace part (or all) of the lawn. Plant native trees, shrubs, grasses, and flowers along the borders of your property as a greenway for animals to travel through, or establish a savanna among oaks and other trees.

I hope to help you create beautiful, delightful, and bountiful Midwestern gardens for yourselves. I believe passionately that we all need to turn our outdoor spaces—public and private—into diverse, sustainable works of art that reflect a unique sense of place.

This book is dedicated to the future and my grandchildren: Thomas, Kristin, Rachel, Sarah, Joseph, and Kathryn.

My liking for gardens to be lavish is an inherent part of my garden philosophy. I like generosity wherever I find it, whether in gardens or elsewhere. I hate to see things scrimp and scrubby. Even the smallest garden can be prodigal within its own limitations.
—V. Sackville-West, *The Illustrated Garden Book*, an Anthology by Robin Lane Fox

Chapter One

ENTRANCE GARDENS

In the suburbs, nature and culture are mingled only by reducing both to a lowest common denominator. In its geometrically perfect form, that denominator is the flat surface, whether black or green. The space that might have been devoted to the intricate play of nature and culture in their higher forms-to woods and paths, duck ponds and produce markets, gardens and cathedrals-is taken up by lawns and parking lots. Together, these make up the flat and neutral playing field on which happiness is pursued.

—Evan Eisenberg, *The Ecology of Eden*

DESIGN FOR A SOUTH-FACING ENTRY GARDEN

MY 1927 SEARS BUNGALOW was the worst house on the block until it was purchased by a rehabber and restored to its former charm. It was love at first sight when I discovered it shortly after it came on the market. All the overgrown junk trees and shrubs had been removed so I had a clean slate to work with. I created an entry garden, but instead of using the typical evergreens, I used native prairie flowers and grasses in my sunny, south-facing front yard.

Blue Wild Indigo (*Baptisia australis*) stands sentinel on either side of the front steps. Tall spires of sapphire-blue pea flowers rise above the smooth, blue-green foliage. The tall, showy spikes rival delphinium for beauty. (Indeed, people walking by my house frequently ask me if my Blue Wild Indigo is delphinium.) It is not, however, temperamental like delphinium—the spires don't need to be staked or cut back at the end of blooming, and the plant doesn't need to be watered, fertilized, or sprayed. Blue Wild Indigo blooms for two to three weeks in mid-May through early June; distinctive dark-gray seedpods follow the flowers in late summer. The foliage remains attractive all through summer and fall and has a shrublike appearance.

An arc of Prairie Dropseed (*Sporobolus heterolepis*) grows along the front foundation under the windows of the glassed-in porch. The whorled, arching mound, 1′ to 2′ tall, is emerald green in spring and summer, turning to coppery bronze in the fall. The delicate, airy panicles of aromatic flowers begin to emerge in August on stiff stems 2′ to 3′ above the foliage; the ripe seed drops by the end of September. This is a splendid

Left: Before—My 1927 Sears bungalow—the worst house on the block

Right: After—The restored house as it looked when I purchased it.

Page xvii: Sparkling white Wild Quinine overlooks front sidewalk to Butterfly Weed in parkway garden

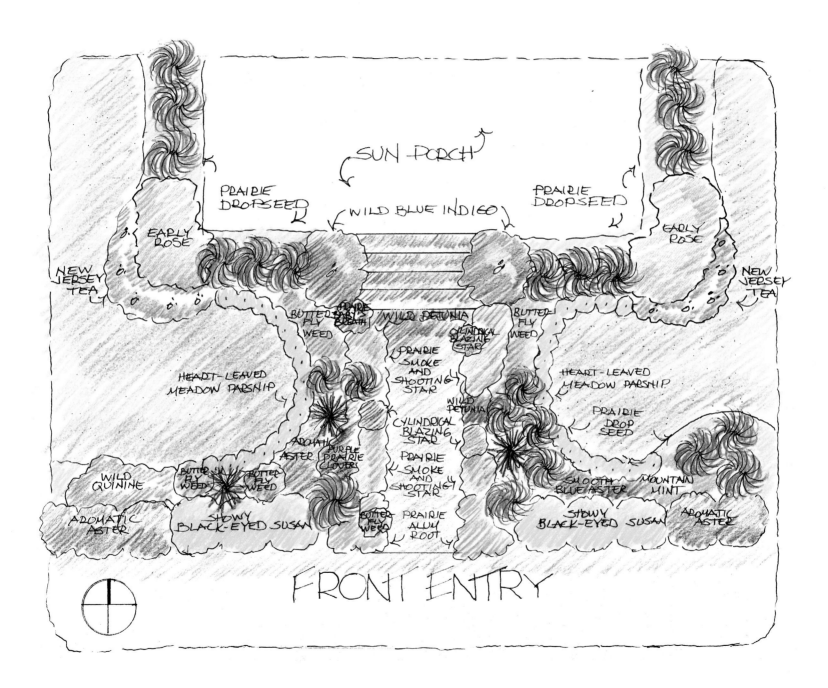

SUN PORCH

PRAIRIE DROPSEED

WILD BLUE INDIGO

PRAIRIE DROPSEED

EARLY ROSE

EARLY ROSE

NEW JERSEY TEA

NEW JERSEY TEA

BUTTER FLY WEED

PRAIRIE BABY'S BREATH

WILD PETUNIA

CYLINDRICAL BLAZING STAR

BUTTER FLY WEED

HEART-LEAVED MEADOW PARSNIP

PRAIRIE SMOKE AND SHOOTING STAR

HEART-LEAVED MEADOW PARSNIP

PRAIRIE DROP SEED

WILD PETUNIA

CYLINDRICAL BLAZING STAR

AROMATIC ASTER

PURPLE PRAIRIE CLOVERS

PRAIRIE SMOKE AND SHOOTING STAR

WILD QUININE

BUTTER FLY WEED

BUTTER FLY WEED

SMOOTH BLUE ASTER

MOUNTAIN MINT

AROMATIC ASTER

SHOWY BLACK-EYED SUSAN

BUTTER FLY WEED

PRAIRIE ALUM ROOT

SHOWY BLACK-EYED SUSAN

AROMATIC ASTER

FRONT ENTRY

Two years later: Native prairie flowers and grasses make a welcoming entrance garden.

Early Wild Rose stretches around the front corner of the porch. Single pink blossoms cover the smooth branches in late May and early June.

plant for home gardens. Situate it under windows, or next to a porch or along a walkway in order to drink in its delightful fragrance (some say it reminds them of buttered popcorn).

Early Wild Rose (*Rosa blanda*) anchors the front corners of the house. The first native rose to bloom, beginning mid-May, it bears 2″, single, pale pink blossoms at the end of nearly thornless, red branches on a shrub 3′ to -5′ tall. Shiny red hips follow the blossoms in late summer and hang on for most of the winter. The leaves turn to apricot and plum in autumn.

Low-growing plants form a colorful tapestry in the beds on either side of the front entry walk. Mats of spring-blooming, coral pink Prairie Smoke (*Geum triflorum*) are stunning for several weeks. Its 8″ stems bear a trio of upright, urn-shaped, rosy flower buds that rise above a clump of toothed, fernlike basal leaves in late March or early April. A few weeks

later, five narrow bracts open like a star from the middle of the now nodding buds. Then in May and June, it gets even better —the buds open wide and spill out misty, feathery mauve plumes up to 2″ long, which give it a hazy, smoky appearance and its common name. Less than a foot tall, it spreads by rhizomes, making it a superb groundcover in sunny, dry areas.

The meandering Prairie Smoke is punctuated with Shooting Star (*Dodecatheon media*). The nodding flowers with reflexed, light or dark pink petals surrounding a black-circled yellow beak do indeed resemble shooting stars, or, less romantically, badminton shuttlecocks. The flowers rise on an 8″ to 12″ stalk above a rosette of smooth, red-tinged, dark green, lance-shaped basal leaves. The leaves and flowers disappear by summer, leaving only the dried stalk. These versatile Shooting Stars are found in prairies, savannas, or calcareous fens.

Left: I get more compliments on my Wild Blue Indigo than any other plant. THe cobalt blue flowers are stunning in May and June. Prairie Smoke blooms at its feet.

Above right: The rosy blossoms of Prairie Smoke contrast delightfully with the golden flowers of Heart-leaved Meadow Parsnip along the entrance walk in spring.

Below right: Shooting Stars (*Dodecatheon media*) punctuate the meandering Prairie Smoke..

The lush creamy-yellow racemes of Cream Wild Indigo join Prairie Smoke.

Cream Wild Indigo (*Baptisia leucophaea*) was placed in front of the Blue Wild Indigo. The pictures I had seen of this plant didn't begin to do it justice. It was like no other plant I had ever seen before—neither words nor photographs adequately describe it. Long, lush, drooping racemes of large, butter-yellow pea blossoms decorate a bushy, rounded mound 2′ tall and wide, of smooth stems and waxy leaves from early to mid-May through early June. It grows in mesic, dry, or sand prairies or in the partial shade of open savannas. I have three of these plants in my gardens—it grows best where it gets morning shade and afternoon sun. Cream Wild Indigo is one of my very favorite plants, but, alas, it's difficult to find in commerce since it seems terribly susceptible to crop failure.

I outlined the inside curve of the beds with Heart-leaved Meadow Parsnip (*Zizia aptera*). The shimmering yellow, flat-topped, umbellate blossoms bloom at the top of 1′ to 3′ stems from mid-April until the end of May, contrasting delightfully with the rosy-pink spring-blooming flowers.

Wild Petunia spills over the edges of the walk in a froth of azure blue in July and August, joined a little later by self-seeded Showy Black-eyed Susan and then Cylindrical Blazing Star. Self-seeded Prairie Dropseed and Little Bluestem add grace to both sides of the walk. A triangle of Prairie Alum Root fills in the corners where the entry walk meets the public sidewalk. This sidewalk is alive with color all season long. May brings clumps of Ohio Spiderwort and Bicknell's Sedge. Wild Quinine and Butterfly Weed are the next to bloom, followed shortly by Pale Purple Coneflower and Stiff Coreopsis for spectacular blooming in late June and early July. The white flowers of Wild Quinine (*Parthenium integrifolium*) grow in a flat-topped cluster at the top of 11/2′ to 4′-tall stems. It puts on a longer show than any other prairie flower, looking as fresh in August as it does in June. Butterfly Weed (*Asclepias tuberosa*), so-named because of its attractiveness to monarchs and other butterflies, is one of the most conspicuous flowers of the prairie. It forms a 1′ to 2′ stiff, upright clump of vibrant orange, flat-topped flower clusters that grows wider and showier every year. If happy, it will seed itself about. The radiant golden-yellow daisy flowers of Prairie or Stiff Coreopsis (*Coreopsis palmata*) bloom at the top of 1′ to 3′ stiff stems. Spreading by rhizomes, it makes luminous patches of sunshine throughout dry or sandy prairies from mid-June into early July. Its unique, narrow, stiff leaves divide in the middle into a trident. Pale Purple Coneflower (*Echinacea pallida*) is similar to the more familiar July-blooming Purple Coneflower, but it has narrower and, more reflexed petals that are a lighter,

Native Americans used the bristly cone of Pale Purple Coneflower to comb their hair.
—Shirley Shirley, *Restoring the Tallgrass Prairie*

Left: Pale Purple Coneflower is taller and the petals are more reflexed than the more familiar Purple Coneflower.

Right: Stiff Coreopsis and Butterfly Weed bring sunshine into the garden in late June through early July.

Lavender-blue Wild Petunia sprawls over the entry walk joined by self-seeded Showy Black-eyed Susan and Yellow Coneflower. The dried stalks of Prairie Alum Root are still apparent.

brighter pink. It also grows taller, up to 40″, and has narrower leaves.

Showy Black-eyed Susan begins to bloom in mid-July and doesn't quit until mid-September. (See Sunny Entrance Garden for description)

Rosy-purple Rough Blazing Star (*Liatris aspera*) is sprinkled throughout the border. The blossoms begin to open at the top of the stem in mid- to late August and continue with a spectacular show well into September. Its flower tufts spill out of large cups arranged in an open fashion alternately around the 1′ to 3′ stem. Blazing Stars grow from corms, in the manner of a crocus; in wet winters and springs the corms indigenous to dry situations sometimes rot—I seem to lose a few plants of Rough Blazing Star every spring. It doesn't seem to make much of a difference though; last September I counted 71 flowering stalks of Rough Blazing Star.

Finally, asters and Little Bluestem take center stage in September and October. Aromatic Aster (*Aster oblongifolius*) forms a 2′ to 3′ soft billowing mound covered with 1½″ daisies with pointed, deep-violet rays and yellow discs that bloom over a long period of time, from mid-September through the end of October. Indigenous to hill prairies, it is rare in the wild; nevertheless, it flourishes in my gardens, spreading quickly by rhizomes and seeds. It does, however, need a well-drained situation—it won't survive in clay soil.

The leafy, blue-green, linear foliage of the Heath Aster (*Aster ericoides*) is indeed heathlike. Tiny, golden-centered white stars form dense plumes at the top of stiff 1′ to 3′ stems in September and October. It grows not only in dry to mesic prairies, but along roadsides and railroad tracks. In the poor, dry soil along railroad tracks it grows into a dainty clump less

Above: Showy Black-eyed Susan blooms along the front sidewalk in July and August.

Below: Fountain-like Prairie Dropseed grows under porch windows.

Aromatic Aster softens the edges of the sidewalk in October. The copper stems of Little Blue Stem enhance the violet flowers of the aster while the chocolate brown seed heads of the self-sown Showy Black-eyed Susan punctuate the entire border.

Left: The leaning rosy spikes of Rough Blazing Star contrast with he rounded blossoms of Mountain Mint and various asters.

Right: The feathery seeds of Little Blue Stem sparkle like diamonds in the autumn sunlight.

than 1′ tall; after observing this, I used it for an edging in my garden, but in rich garden soil it grows 3′ tall! It increases primarily by rhizomes and seed.

The 2′ to 3′ stiff leaves and stems of Little Bluestem (*Andropogon scoparius*) have a decided bluish cast in spring and summer—some more than others. Flower spikes emerge from the axils of the leaf and stem in July and begin to bloom in August, the inconspicuous pale-yellow stigmas and plum-colored anthers emanating directly out of the spikelets. But while the flowers themselves are hardly noticeable, they soon turn into dazzling white feathery seeds that catch the light and sparkle like diamonds on the now-copper stems throughout the fall and winter.

A front entry walk need not be concrete as mine is. It will be even more inviting if constructed of flagstone or brick—perhaps curved instead of straight. A vine-covered trellis at the sidewalk juncture will increase its appeal and importance even more.

There is color in this small garden from the first Prairie Smoke in spring, through the asters in fall. The *Baptisia* pods are notable throughout the fall and winter, while Prairie Dropseed, Little Bluestem, and Prairie Alum Root provide foliage interest all year. ❧

DESIGN FOR A PARKWAY GARDEN
Sunny Site, Well-drained Soil

BRAND-NEW, CHEERFUL, lavender-blue flared trumpets of Wild Petunia (*Ruellia humilis*) greet the dawn every morning. The lavender-blue trumpet blossoms do indeed resemble the annual petunias we're familiar with, but they are smaller and not as flared. The flowers open before the dawn and close by afternoon on hot summer days. In light shade or on cooler days, the blossoms last all day. A sprawling plant, the gray-green foliage billows and puffs over the edge of the front entry walk and along all my sidewalks and among the flagstones in the back terrace. Not the least of the charms of this plant is its penchant for seeding itself with reckless abandon—within the stones of the patio, along the edges of the garden where there's still a bit of bare dirt, and in the newly created gardens. Then

one day, petunia blossoms appeared in the lawn in the front parkway! First just one, then a sprinkling as the week wore on. I finally had to mow the lawn and with it the petunias, but within a few days, they were blooming again.

By the third year, thick patches crowded out the grass, so I began to mow around rather than over them. Some small Showy Black-eyed Susan began to bloom within the petunias, as well; then Smooth Blue and Aromatic Aster appeared; subsequently, a couple of Butterfly Weeds also made the area their home.

As abundantly as the above plants grew, Kentucky bluegrass still appeared within the garden. Wild Petunia is late to emerge from the ground in the spring. I took advantage of this trait and herbicided the bluegrass that grew within the bed; I

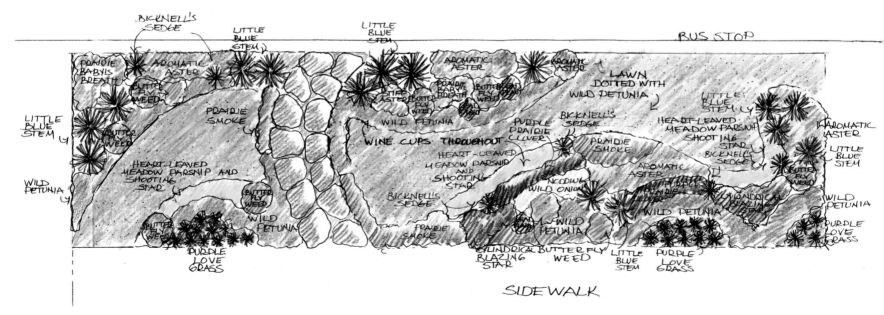

Above left: Self-seeded patches of WIld Petunia grow throughout the parkway.

Above right: Wild Petunia combines with Purple Prairie Clover and Wine Cups in July.

Below left: Showy Wine Cups weave through the garden, in bloom all summer.

Below right: Fringed purple tutus of Purple Prairie Clover bloom with Butterfly Weed in July.

The airy blossoms of Prairie Baby's Breath add a delicate note to any garden in July and August.

Left: It is apparent why this plant is called the Nodding Wild Onion.

Right: Pale Purple Coneflower and Wlld Quinine overlook Butterfly Weed in parkway.

also extended the garden toward the corner.

After the grass died and the Wild Petunia emerged, I created my garden with a mixture of low-growing plants. Bloom begins in May, echoing the front walk, with Prairie Smoke, Shooting Star, Heart-leaved Meadow Parsnip, and Bicknell's Sedge. Mid- to late June brings Pale Purple Coneflower and Butterfly Weed. The radiant fuchsia cups of Wine Cups (*Callirhoe involucrata*), also called Purple Poppy Mallow, bloom all summer on relaxed hairy stems that weave through the garden. An immigrant from the west, it thrives in hot, dry situations. Wild Petunia, which started it all, joins the mix, its carpet of lavender-blue blossoms a perfect foil for the vibrancy of the still-blooming Butterfly Weed and Wine Cups.

Purple Prairie Clover (*Petalostemum purpureum*) begins to bloom in early July. A purple-fringed tutu of blossoms climbs up the tubular cone and becomes a long purple cylinder as the season progresses. Bright-purple-stemmed, golden-orange anthers dot the purple petals-a stunning contrast. It grows 1′ to 3′ tall on stiff stems with sparse, compound, needlelike leaves.

Prairie Baby's Breath (*Euphorbia corollata*) or Flowering Spurge, its more commonly used name, joins the mix in early July, as well. It does, indeed, resemble the more familiar Baby's Breath (*Gypsophila paniculata*) of florist's bouquets and old-fashioned gardens. Its erect, 1′- to 3′-tall stems branch out near the top, then again and again, forming a flat-topped corymb of dainty, five-petaled white flowers that lend an airy note to any garden in July and August. Although it appears to be quite delicate, it is a common, hardy plant found not only in sandy, dry, and mesic prairies, but also along railroad tracks and in pastures.

Late July brings the pink globes of Nodding Wild Onion (*Allium cernuum*). Sharply nodding, leafless stems rise

Nodding Wild Onion in bloom.

The wanton Aromatic Aster has seeded itself liberally throughout the parkway and provides the final show of the season.

18″ from long, flat, narrow, onion-like basal leaves. Then clusters of individual, tiny bells form a globe at the end of the stems, white at first, then becoming pink and rose as they age.

A haze of red-violet wispy flowers of Purple Love Grass (*Eragrostis spectabilis*) make a delightful attendant to the lavender-blue trumpets of Wild Petunia. It blooms 1 to-1^1/$_2$′ above compact clumps of foliage from early August through September. Common in sandy soils, even railroad ballast, it requires a dry, well-drained situation in full sun.

While Kentucky Blue Grass lawns become dormant and turn brown during the heat and drought of July and August, these prairie plants never falter—indeed, once established, they thrive on sunny days where temperatures are 90° or more, even with no rainfall. ✎

DESIGN FOR A SUNNY ENTRANCE GARDEN

A FEW YEARS AGO, a spectacular house was built on the edge of a bluff overlooking the Fox River in the town where I live. In keeping with the natural site, the owner planted native woodland wildflowers in the tree-shaded, steeply-sloped back yard and created a prairie garden in the flat, south-facing, sunny front yard—the first in town. Much of the garden was sensational but some plants did not work out well. I re-designed parts of it similar to this plan:

The front entry walk leads from the street to the front porch; in addition, a double walk made of stepping stones meanders from the driveway to the porch. The front walk is lined with large exuberant plants that will be noticed by drivers passing by in the street. Midsummer brings flowers of the sun: golden Stiff Coreopsis and orange Butterfly Weed. Wild

Quinine, Pale Purple Coneflower, and New Jersey Tea join in the tapestry, while Lead Plant and Purple Prairie Clover add their purple blossoms in July. Wild Petunia and Nodding Wild Onion bloom along the verge in July and August. Rough Blazing Star, dotted throughout the garden, begins to bloom in late August, joined by white and lavender asters in September.

The double paver walk outlines an intimate garden of diminutive flowers and grasses, beginning with the spring-blooming Prairie Smoke. A matrix of Prairie Panic Grass (*Panicum leibergii*) fills in a large area. A short bunchgrass with broad, vivid green leaves, its spikelets of shiny round seeds rise above the foliage from June through September. It's combined with a large stand of the delightful Thimbleweed, in bloom in June. Wild Petunia sprawls around the edges of the stepping-

Left: The row of Showy Black-eyed Susan and Prairie Drop Seed are spectacular along the edge of this prairie garden.

Right: Prairie plants become exquisite snow-catchers in winter.

The diminutive Frost Aster blooms the whole month of August. Plant it in an intimate garden in a well-drained site.

stones, beginning in late June, joined in August by the color-ful, airy bloom of Purple Love Grass. Early August also brings the tiny, $3/4'$ white daisies of the Frost or Stiff Aster (*Aster ptarmicoides*). The flowers grow in flat, branching clusters at the top of stiff 12″ to 18″ stems that are clothed with lustrous dark green, willow-like foliage.

The most sensational display of all is the curve of Showy Black-eyed Susan (*Rudbeckia speciosa, var. sullivantii*) and Prairie Dropseed that defines the garden from the walk along the garage to the front walk. Showy Black-eyed Susan is ubiq-uitous in Midwestern landscapes and gardens—it says "Midwest" more than any other flower. The golden-petaled daisies with chocolate-brown centers bloom from mid- to late July until mid-September on a bushy plant 2′ to 3′ tall and up

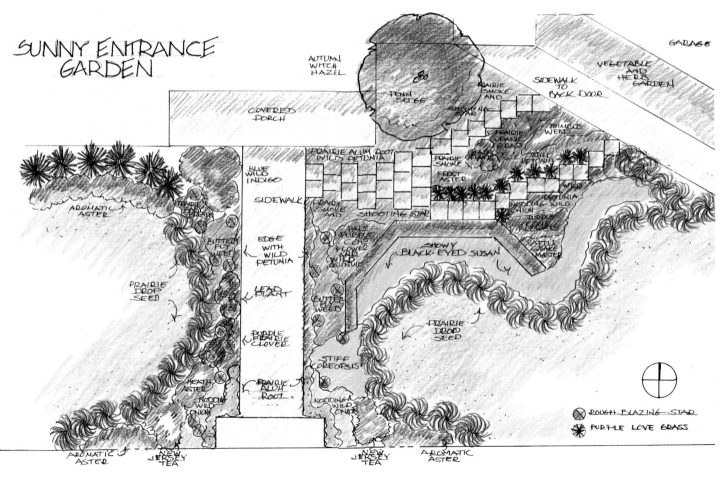

Choose the species over the cultivar—'Goldsturm' is highly susceptible to Botritis Blight, which turns the leaves black and at the very least stops the bloom for the season; at worst, it will kill the plant. The disease is spread by overhead sprinkling or a rainy season.

to 4' wide. Indigenous to calcareous wet habitats, it nevertheless grows well in ordinary garden soil. Because it has a shallow root system, however, it is not drought-resistant—a dry summer will cause severe wilting and even death. Don't plant it in an especially well-drained situation such as in a raised planter or on a hillside—it will wilt every sunny day. Though it is rare in the wild, it is commonly found at nurseries (the popular cultivar 'Goldsturm' is derived from this species). Both the species and the cultivar seed themselves aggressively. You will have an abundance of riches to fill in other areas of your yard plus lots more to give away.

This garden is also spectacular in winter when all the plants become delightful snow-catchers. ❧

Tangerine Butterfly Weed and golden Stiff Coreopsis, flowers of the sun, bloom at Midsummer in this spectacular garden.

DESIGN FOR A FRONT-YARD GARDEN
FOR A TYPICAL NEW HOUSE

THIS IS A TYPICAL NEW subdivision house on a 65′-wide lot, with a 30′- deep front yard. Traditionally, it would be landscaped with a row of yews around the foundation and a shade tree in the middle of the front lawn.

But our goal is to provide a bountiful garden and incidentally to cut the lawn area in half. There are other concerns to address as well: as in most houses built today, the garage is the most prominent feature of the house and has to be somewhat hidden or disguised; in addition, the two-story-high windows on the southwest corner must to be shaded from the afternoon sun. Two judiciously placed shade trees will take care of both problems. Plant the first tree in the small area north of the driveway, which will partially hide the garage so that the first view of the house will be of the front door. Plant another

Wild Petunia and Wine Cups bloom in the small garden at the conjunction of the driveway and sidewalk.

tree just off the corner of the house to shade the windows in the afternoon.

Carve out a half-moon from the corner of the front porch to the driveway edge for a small lawn. The curve of the circle will lead one's eye from the driveway to the front door, just where we want it to go. Place an 'Annabelle' Hydrangea next to the front door and surround it with Nodding Wild Onion; then arrange fragrant Prairie Dropseed next to the front porch. Plant a row of Prairie Alum Root between the sidewalk and the house. Make a slightly mounded bed at the conjunction of the driveway and entry walk and plant it with low-growing flowers and grasses.

Place plants in the area that will eventually be shaded by the canopy of the tree that will prosper in the sun now and then adapt to partial shade later. Next place a bench and chairs under the tree. Houses nowadays are oriented toward backyard living, while the front yard is considered public. But children love to play on the driveway and sidewalks with their wheeled toys, roller skates, and chalk games such as hopscotch. A bench gives Mom a place to sit to supervise children's play; it also makes for a friendlier, safer neighborhood when people are out in front of their houses overlooking the public area.

Create a low berm around the corner of the lot to give a sense of enclosure to the lawn area. Arrange a staggered row of Little Bluestem along the top of the berm; then intermingle patches of Butterfly Weed, Pale Purple Coneflower, Purple Prairie Clover, and Prairie Baby's Breath within the grass for summer bloom. Edge the bed with more Prairie Alum Root.

Big-leaved Aster is a good choice to plant under the trees at the entrance to the stone path next to the garage.

DESIGN FOR A SHADY ENTRANCE GARDEN
Shade, Partial Shade, Medium to Dry Soil

THIS IS A DESIGN FOR A north-facing entry garden of a two-story house that will cast a long shadow over the garden area most of the day.

A pair of Maple-leaved Arrowwood (*Viburnum acerifolium*) defines the front door. Aptly-named, its dark green, trilobed leaves do indeed resemble those of a maple tree. Its flat-topped, yellowish-white flowers open in late May followed by blue-black berries in fall, an attractive contrast to the wine-colored autumn leaves. Horizontally branched, it grows 4′ to 6′ tall. It's one of the best shrubs for dry shade, but it is seldom found at nurseries. Ask for it and it will soon be more widely available.

The horizontally branching pattern of the Apple Service-berry (*Amelanchier x grandiflora*) on either corner ties the house to the ground. A naturally occurring hybrid between Allegheny Shadblow (*Amelanchier laevis*) and Shadbush (*Amelanchier arborea*), it is a multistemmed, upright, shrublike small tree that grows 20′ tall with a 15′ spread. A white cloud of blossoms covers its bare branches in early to mid-April before the downy leaves unfold.

Another name for these delightful trees is Juneberry, referring to the reddish-purple berries produced in abundance in June and July. Similar in taste to a blueberry, they can be eaten out of hand or combined with or used as a substitute for blueberries in pies, jams, muffins, or preserves. Birds relish these berries, especially cardinals and robins.

In fall, the foliage turns to a brilliant crimson. In winter its smooth silvery bark is splendid against the white snow. It is one of the best four-season ornamental trees there is—I can't speak highly enough of it. It is a superb tree to use in the home landscape. Use it to accent a front door or plant a pair at the corners of a house; make it a focal point in a garden or a shrubbery border; or place it in a naturalized situation.

'Annabelle' Hydrangea connects the Viburnum and the Serviceberry. 'Annabelle' is a naturally occurring selection of Smooth Hydrangea (*Hydrangea aborescens*) found near Anna, Illinois. It grows 3′ to 4′ tall on unbranched canes and expands up to 5′ wide. The flower heads of 'Annabelle' are as large as 8″ to 12″ in diameter, compared with a 4″ to 6″ diameter for the species. I think the large, overblown flowers look quite artificial in a naturalistic situation, but their tendency to bend over and flop on the ground gives them a careless look that mitigates the attempt at pretension. In any event, Smooth Hydrangea is a wonderful plant for July bloom, either as part of a naturalized woodland situation or a more formal planting. Group them under tall trees, plant a pair on either side of a partially shaded front door, or string an informal hedge around a north- or east-facing porch. (Cut back the stems of older plants to a height of 12″ to 15″ in early spring to keep them compact.)

The blossoms progress from green to white, back to green, and then turn to brown in October. Pick them at any stage-they're a flower arranger's delight whether the blossoms are fresh or dried. I've combined dried 'Annabelle' Hydrangea, Northern Sea Oats, and Switch Grass in cool green half-vases on the walls of my porch. Indigenous to sandstone cliffs, Smooth Hydrangea is abundant in Starved Rock State Park in

Above left: The large snowball flowers of 'Annabelle' Hydrangea are stunning in July and August.

Above right: 'Gro-low' Sumac makes a spectacular groundcover in sun or shade.

Below left: The large, rose-purple blossoms of Purple Flowering Raspberry are exceptionally showy in late June and July.

Below right: The showy, fragrant blossoms of Illinois Rose appear in late June– early July.

HOUSE

'ANNABELLE' HYDRANGEA

ANNAB...

MAPLE-LEAVED VIBURNUM

LONG-BEAKED SEDGE

SERVICE BERRY

GRO-LOW SUMAC

PRAIRIE ALUM ROOT

LAWN WITH SPRING BEAUTY TOOTHWORT COMMON CINQUEFOIL EARLY BUTTERCUP WILD STRAWBER...

PURPLE FLOWERING RASPBERRY

ILLINOIS ROSE

LITTLE BLUE STEM

SHADY ENTRY GARDEN

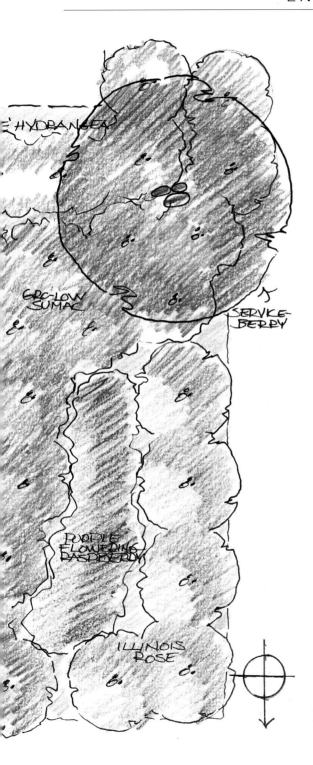

Illinois and at Turkey Run State Park in Indiana. It is not drought-tolerant, however; it will need supplementary water in dry summers.

'Gro-Low' Sumac (*Rhus aromatica* 'Gro-Low') carpets the area in front of the hydrangeas, sweeps under the Serviceberry, and outlines the shrubbery border up to the front sidewalk. A cultivar of Fragrant Sumac, only 2′ high with a spread of 6′ to 8′, it makes an excellent ground cover for large areas. The pleasantly aromatic, glossy green summer foliage intermittently becomes scarlet, burgundy, and gold in mid-October; then it turns an all-over warm vermilion by the end of the month, usually persisting through mid-November.

The Illinois Rose, also called Prairie Rose or Michigan Rose (*Rosa setigera*), travels along the edge of the property and fills in the front corners. It is the latest-blooming and showiest of our native roses. Abundant clusters of fragrant, deep-pink blossoms, $2^{1/2}″$ wide, centered with golden stamens, cover the heavily armed canes from late June through mid-July. Lustrous dark green, ovate leaflets, arranged in threes, turn to brilliant scarlet and orange in the fall. Cherry-red, $^{1/2}″$ round hips ripen in September and last through much of the winter. It grows 5′ to 6′ tall and across; its red-green canes grow vigorously and may be trained up a trellis. This rose is found in the wild along woodland edges and in savanna openings, frequently with Iowa Crab and Wild Plum.

Illinois Rose was a favorite of both Wilhelm Miller and Jens Jensen. Wilhelm Miller wanted everyone in Illinois to plant one next to their front door as a symbol of their commitment to the native flora of Illinois. Jens Jensen used it extensively in his designs, particularly along fences or spilling over limestone ledges.

The scarlet fall foliage of Serviceberry is spectacular.

In central Indiana the prairie rose runs over farm fences, along the roadside hedges, and in the open glades of the woodlands. Wherever it grows it is a lovely bouquet, and its red berries over the snow in winter are as colorful as the rose in June.

—Jens Jensen, *Sifting*

I was enchanted by the beauty of the Purple Flowering Raspberry (*Rubus odoratus*) I the first time I saw it blooming at the Chicago Botanic Garden. Loose clusters of 2″ rose-purple saucers filled with pale golden stamens appear in June and continue through July and sporadically into August. Small, flat, red raspberries follow in August and September—regrettably, not as juicy or sweet as our Black Raspberries. Like all native shrubs, it has visual interest for more than one season—its large, maple-like leaves turn to gold in autumn, while the slowly colonizing, 3′ to 6′ tall, arching, thornless stems have attractive exfoliating bark, especially notable in winter. Purple-flowering Raspberry also provides food and shelter for wildlife. It fills in the area between the 'Gro-low' Sumac and the Illinois Rose.

A central walk, outlined with Prairie Alum Root, cuts through the circular lawn, which is scattered with patches of low-growing early wildflowers. The delicate, lime-green bells of Prairie Alum Root (*Heuchera richardsonii*) are arranged in clusters of two or three near the top of 2′-tall stems that rise from a robust clump of geranium-shaped basal leaves, creating an airy note from mid-May to late June. They are not as colorful as Coral Bells, their Rocky Mountain cousins, but nevertheless provocative orange tongues stick out from the center of their bells in May. The robust leaves turn to a lovely burgundy in fall, which lasts through most of the winter.

Fountains of Long-beaked Sedge grow next to the front steps; clumps of Little Bluestem define the conjuncture with the public sidewalk.

This is not meant to be a manicured garden with sheared shrubs. This garden is dynamic, with varying interest all year. These shrubs might be considered somewhat untidy, but they will be ravishing throughout the year with flowers, berries, colorful fall foliage, and attractive bark. ❦

Native Americans mixed the berries of the Amelanchier with fat and dried buffalo meat to make pemmican cakes, portable meals that provided nutrition during winter travels.

FRAGRANCE IN THE PRAIRIE GARDEN

FRAGRANCE ISN'T MUCH OF A FACTOR in the prairie garden, and I miss it. Oh, there's vanilla-scented Sweet Grass and milkweeds and the Joe Pye Weeds; and then there are various wild roses with a typically sweet rose fragrance; and, of course, the mints: Wild Bergamot, Mountain Mint, and especially Wild Mint. But I long for the old-fashioned scents in the garden that take us back to childhood, such as that of lily-of-the-valley, lilac, peony, and phlox. But only the phlox is native to America.

Spring-blooming Wild Blue Phlox has a delightful fragrance, but Garden Phlox is even sweeter, especially those with white flowers. Phlox seeds itself liberally—in July and August, older gardens that have been "let go" are filled almost exclusively with luscious fuchsia, lavender, white, and calico phlox. While Garden Phlox is native principally to the southeastern United States, the Chicago region is in its "alleged natural range" according to Swink and Wilhelm's *Plants of the Chicago Region.*

Smells detonate softly in our memory like poignant land mines, hidden under the weedy mass of many years and experiences. Hit a tripwire of smell, and memories explode all at once.
—Diane Ackerman, *Natural History of the Senses*

Phlox, an American genus, with countless species from mountains, prairies and woodlands, includes the August-blooming Phlox paniculata that brings a unique scent to the late summer garden. No perennial, no fragrance, so typifies the month of August as does summer phlox. The old wild forms have the most pronounced odor, the small-flowered whites and calicoes, rosy lavender and magenta. We shall always remember a sunny city garden, just a square plot, jammed with clumps of these and lavender bergamot, Monarda fistulosa, while over them swung the spotted pink turkscap of rubrum lilies.
—Helen van Pelt Wilson and Leonie Bell, *The Fragrant Year*

DESIGN FOR A COTTAGE GARDEN
Sun, Partial Sun, Medium Soil

THIS FRONT-DOOR "COTTAGE GARDEN" is based on one I designed for a client who was particularly fond of Bee Balm. She requested a color scheme of pinks and purples, so I filled the area with cultivars of Bee Balm and Garden Phlox; I then added Purple Coneflower and the tall spires of Prairie Blazing Star. Broad-leaved Purple Coneflower (*Echinacea purpurea*) is a familiar, old-fashioned flower that has been a staple in Midwestern gardens since settlement days. While the bold rose-purple daisy with a large, copper-brown center cone is common in "wildflower" mixes, and its cultivars are notably popular at garden centers, it is rare in the wild. It is sometimes found along railroad tracks, but is more likely to appear in Bur Oak savannas. In a home garden it grows 3′ to 4′ tall and spreads by rhizomes and seeds.

Prairie Blazing Star or Kansas Gayfeather (*Liatris pycnostachya*) is one of the most conspicuous inhabitants of the prairie. Dense fuchsia flower spikes bloom from late July to mid-August on 2′- to 5′-tall, stiff, unbranched stems clad with linear leaves. Like all members of the genus *Liatris*, the flower spikes start to bloom from the top down instead of from the bottom up, as most other spike flowers do.

Subsequently, I introduced shimmering white spikes of 'Husker Red' Foxglove Beard Tongue with burgundy foliage and stems, tall white candelabras of Culver's Root, and airy sprays of sparkling white Prairie Baby's Breath. Three spectacular rose-colored 'Super Rose' Rose Mallow, cultivars of the

Left: Bee Balm (*Monarda didyma*) cultivars come in shades of purple, pink, and red.

Right: The flowers of Purple Coneflower and a 'Super Rose' Rose Mallow are a contrast in size.

This spectacular garden of Purple Joe Pye Weed, 'Jacob Cline' Beebalm, 'Super Rose' Rose Mallow, and Purple Coneflower picks up the rosy -purple color of the house trim in July and August.

. . . sweet as summer.   **—Shakespeare,** *Henry VIII*

native Swamp Rose Mallow (*Hibiscus palustris*), become focal points in late summer. Joe Pye Weed grows at intervals next to the porch pillars. Three clumps of red-bladed 'Shenandoah' Switch Grass stand sentinel on either side of the front door; dusty pink Prairie Smoke puffs and billows next to the entry walk. Swirling clumps of Prairie Dropseed fill in the corners, travel along the verge, eventually joining Prairie Alum Root. Purple, lavender, and pink asters follow the summer display, while 'Gro-low' Sumac provides the green background. ❧

This garden faces east with morning sun and afternoon shade.

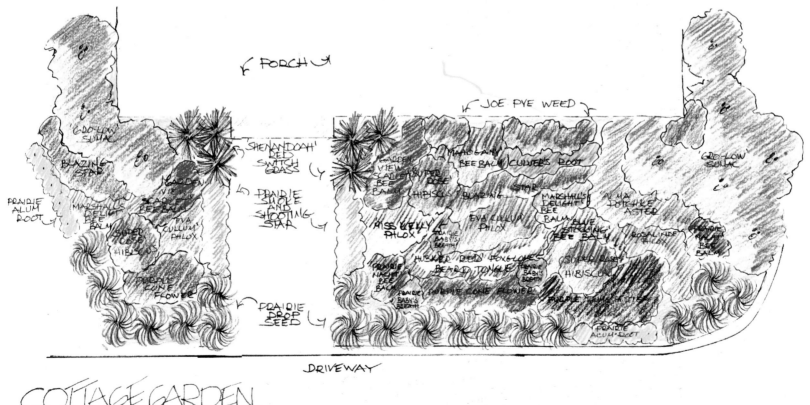

page 35

DESIGN FOR A WALK-THROUGH FRONT GARDEN
Sun, Medium Soil

A FLAGSTONE PATH wound its way through a perennial garden in front of this house to a side deck. But after attending a slide-lecture about gardening with native plants that I gave at The Natural Garden, a perennial plant nursery in St. Charles, Illinois, the gardener decided she wanted to use native plants in her garden to make it more nature friendly and, not incidentally, give it more pizzazz.

We left a few favorite plants the owner wanted to keep, but replaced the rest with native prairie forbs and grasses.

Asters, grasses, and the foliage of the Serviceberry bring color in September, October, and even beyond. The silver bark of the Serviceberry, graceful grasses, seedpods, cones, and the dried inflorescences of the forbs create a striking winter presentation. ❧

Spotted Joe Pye Weed, Purple Coneflower, Wild Quinine, Nodding Wild Onion, Prairie Baby's Breath, and Rattlesnake Master bloom with the previously planted Red Beebalm in July in the walk-through garden.

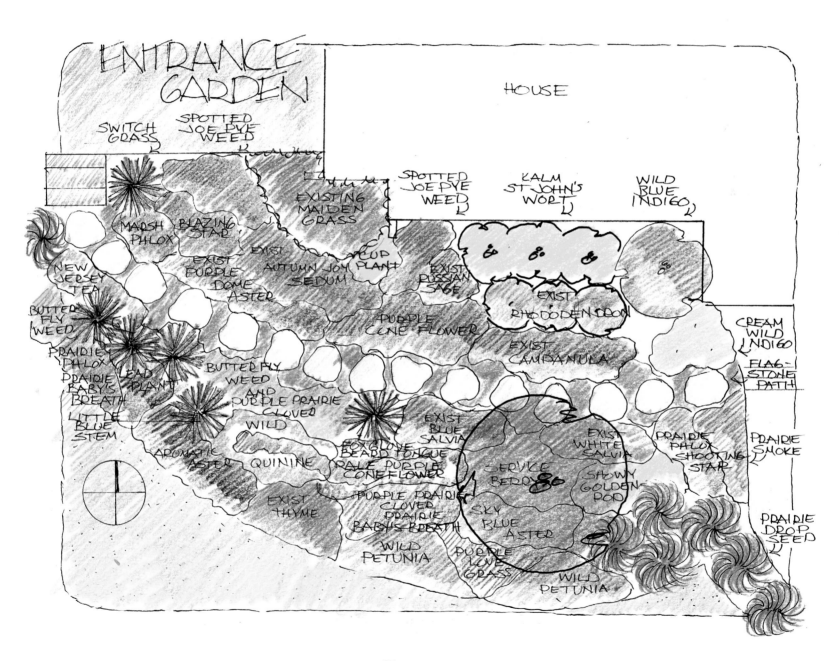

TERRACE TAPESTRY
Sun, Part Sun, Dry to Medium Soil

DECKS ARE ALL THE RAGE NOW, having supplanted the Spartan concrete-slab patios that were standard issue for sub-division houses in the 60s and 70s. Decks, however, raise you above the garden; and while you can oversee your domain, you cannot interact with the garden. Attractive as decks are, consider building a brick or flagstone terrace instead of, or in addition to, a deck. Sitting amid the flowers you will experience the sensuous fragrance, color, and texture in far more detail than if you observe them from afar.

A brick or stone terrace is even more attractive when various flowers fill in the cracks and open spaces. That situation might be considered inhospitable, but on the contrary, many plants prefer a site where their roots can develop in the sandy coolness under rocks. If you have flowers growing next to your terrace, you will notice their seedlings springing up in the cracks within a year. I had a brick terrace at my townhouse that had a wonderful assortment of self-sown flowers—Lady's Mantle, Iceberg Sedum, Veronica, Tiger Lily, Wild Geranium, and Common Blue Violet. Only the Wild Geranium and Violets were native plants, but this situation will fit many other indigenous plants.

More recently, after I bought my Sears bungalow, I had a flagstone terrace installed between my house and garage: a 12-foot circle in partial to full sun and an adjacent 7-foot circle that was in the shade. The flagstone was laid on a base of limestone screenings and the cracks between the stones were filled in with a sand and soil mixture. I gleaned a list of native plants that particularly appreciate limestone from Swink and Wilhelm's *Plants of the Chicago Region*.

The first to bloom in sunnier areas of the terrace in April is the Pasque Flower (*Anemone patens*), followed by Shooting Star in May. The large, pale-lavender cups with golden centers of the Pasque Flowers rise above downy, segmented leaves. Similar to Prairie Smoke, the blossoms turn to long, silky plumes. Pasque Flower is rare in Illinois and Iowa, found only occasionally in rocky or gravelly hill prairies. They are more abundant in the sand counties of Wisconsin. "Only gravel ridges are poor enough to offer pasques full elbow-room in April sun. They endure snows, sleets, and bitter winds for the privilege of blooming alone," says Aldo Leopold in *A Sand County Almanac*. Mine lasted several years, but eventually they petered out and I have not replaced them.

The common Blue Violet nestles within the attractive spotted foliage of Virginia Waterleaf in the shady areas of the terrace in May. The white star flowers of Wild Stonecrop (*Sedum ternatum*), a native sedum, which grows between the stones of both terraces, is the next to bloom. Growing in sun or partial shade, it is indigenous to limestone bluffs and rock canyons. While it grows abundantly for me next to and around flagstones, it hasn't survived in clients' gardens in the same situation. Wild Columbine's favorite place to grow is among rocks, so it is extremely happy here in both the sunny and shadier parts of the terrace. It seeds itself prolifically; by September, there were numerous seedlings scattered about.

June-blooming Thimbleweed (*Anemone cylindrica*) grows along the edges of the patio. Greenish-white, petal-like sepals surround a thimble that elongates as the flowers fade, which gives it its common name (another name for it is Candle

Thimbleweed or Candle Anemone is at home in dry prairies—be sure to plant it in well-drained soil. It blooms in May.

Page 38: The silky, lavender Pasque Flower is the first prairie flower to bloom, in April.

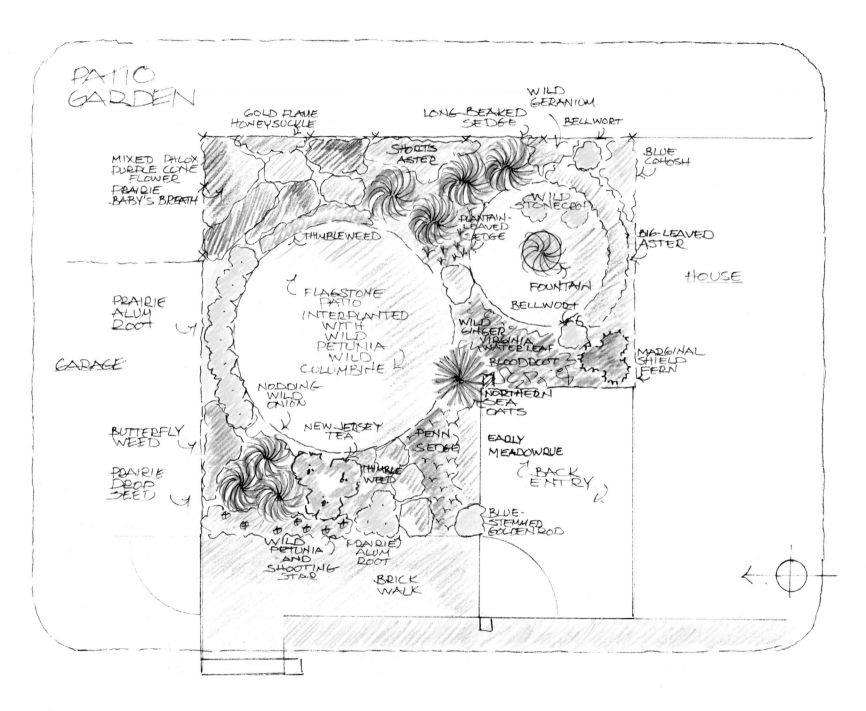

PATIO GARDEN

GOLD FLAME HONEYSUCKLE

LONG BEAKED SEDGE

WILD GERANIUM

BELLWORT

MIXED PHLOX PURPLE CONE FLOWER
PRAIRIE BABY'S BREATH

SHORTIS ASTER

BLUE COHOSH

THIMBLEWEED

PLANTAIN-LEAVED SEDGE

WILD STONECROP

BIG-LEAVED ASTER

FLAGSTONE PATIO
INTERPLANTED WITH WILD PETUNIA WILD COLUMBINE

FOUNTAIN

BELLWORT

HOUSE

PRAIRIE ALUM ROOT

WILD GINGER
VIRGINIA WATER LEAF
BLOODROOT

MARGINAL SHIELD FERN

GARAGE

NODDING WILD ONION

NORTHERN SEA OATS

NEW JERSEY TEA

PENN SEDGE

EARLY MEADOWRUE

BUTTERFLY WEED

THIMBLE WEED

BACK ENTRY

PRAIRIE DROP SEED

BLUE-STEMMED GOLDENROD

WILD PETUNIA AND SHOOTING STAR

PRAIRIE ALUM ROOT

BRICK WALK

Anemone). The 1″-wide flowers bloom in June on long stems above a whorl of five-parted leaves. Its seed fluff hangs on all winter; in spring it is treasured by hummingbirds for nesting material. Or you can scatter the seed—it will bloom the second year after sowing. It grows in sun or partial shade.

In the sunniest area of the garden, next to the south garage wall, Butterfly Weed and New Jersey Tea bloom in June and July; Prairie Drop Seed adds interest all year.

Wild Petunia sprawls along the edges and among the stones of the sunny patio, blooming in July and August. It is also a good choice to grow along a path or sidewalk. The lavender-blue color contrasts especially well with terra-cotta brick walkways or terraces. A prolific seeder, it will soon fill up the cracks between the stones. In the third summer, small plants of Butterfly Weed and Culver's Root appeared in the cracks, as well. The pink globes of Nodding Wild Onion bloomed along the verge with the Wild Petunia, a pretty combination.

The narrow area between my patio and privacy fence proved to be the most difficult aspect of all to grow prairie plants. While English perennial borders cry out for a background such as a fence, wall, or hedge, the motto of prairie flowers and grasses seems to be "Don't fence me in." All the many different plants I tried leaned away from the wall and eventually flopped over. (I also had problems with tall plants grown next to house walls that inevitably fell over.) The truth is that prairie plants don't like to grow next to walls. The internodes of plants grown in the shade stretch longer than the internodes of plants grown in the sun; therefore, the side of the plant next to the wall, being shaded, will become longer than the front of the stem which is in full sun. As the back of the stem grows longer than the front of the stem, it curves, and eventually it falls over. It, of

Above: Shooting Star grows in sun or partial shade. It blooms in May.

Below: Wild Columbine has seeded itself within the stones of the patio.

Left: Various Phlox cultivars, Purple Coneflower, Purple Joe Pye Weed, and Prairie Baby's Breath bloom in corner of patio next to the fence.

Above right: Clumps of Wild Stonecrop spill out between the flagstones in the shady part of the patio. In the foreground, Wild Columbine is about to bloom.

Below right: The patio table and chairs are situated in a sea of flowers. Wild Petunia and Nodding Wild Onion grow and bloom within the flagstones in July and August.

course, makes perfect sense. (Cultivated plants have had that characteristic bred out of them.)

The other problem I had was that the space between my patio and fence was in the root zone and under the canopy of a Black Walnut tree that prevented the growth of some plants.

I transplanted the Blazing Star, Tall Coreopsis, Culver's Root, Foxglove Beard Tongue, and Smooth Blue Aster that I first planted there to more open areas, where they now stand upright. The Purple Coneflower next to the fence was doing well, so I left it there. I added several clumps of pink, lavender, calico, and white cultivated Garden Phlox along with Prairie Baby's Breath, Starry Campion, Wild Bergamot, and Purple Giant Hyssop. In September, the area is taken over by a blue haze of self-sown Short's Aster and a few golden Blue-stemmed Goldenrod. Short's Aster blooms from late August to mid-October above long, arrow-shaped leaves. A prolific seeder, its progeny will grow and flower within the stones in three years.

I then added a copper fountain, visible from the patio and my studio window, to add even more sensuous pleasure. You will have to watch where you walk or place furniture on a terrace that's filled with plants peeking or billowing out from between the stones, but this design creates an extremely pleasant place to just sit and enjoy not only the flowers, but also the bees and butterflies they attract. ❧

MOSS

Soft green mats of moss are lovely growing in the cracks of brick or stone terraces that are situated in the shade. Moss will establish itself on its own, but you can enhance the process, according to Rick Anderson of Stone Works in Columbia, South Carolina. He shared these formulas with us at a lecture at the Chicago Botanic Garden in January 1996:

➤ If moss is already growing in an area, paint it with buttermilk to make it grow more luxuriantly.

➤ If there is no moss at all, mix up a concoction of one bottle of beer, $1/2$ cup of sugar, and a handful of moss in a blender; then pour it between the cracks of the terrace's stones or bricks.

You can also use either process to paint on new clay pots to "age" them instantly. ❧

DESIGN FOR A SUNNY BACKYARD WITH ROSES AND PERGOLAS
Full Sun, Medium to Dry-Medium Soil

LOCATE THIS GARDEN in an open area such as the end of a backyard that is well away from the shade cast by large trees or buildings. Place the Serviceberries on the north side of the garden so they won't cast shade on the garden.

A path journeys under an arbor that leads to a round stone or brick patio encircled by a row of Prairie Alum Root. Arrange terra-cotta pots of grasses and forbs or herbs on the stones, and/or place a sundial or other ornament in the center of the circle. The path flows out the opposite side to a bench situated in front of a row of Serviceberry trees underplanted with undulating waves of 'Gro-low' Sumac.

The corner beds next to the bench feature early summer flowers, while the other two beds flanking the entrance are filled with late summer blooms. Raise the beds with flagstone curbs or level them with the lawn. A lawn is contained in each segment between the patio and the flowerbeds. Plant Buffalo Grass or Prairie Panic Grass instead of turf grass if the soil is sufficiently well drained. Sprinkle the grass with small bulbs such as Shooting Star, Nodding Wild Onion, and Cylindrical Blazing Star, plus flowers such as Common Cinquefoil, Wild Petunia, and Cynthia.

Two paths, which may be built of flagstone, brick, or crushed gravel, lead away from the patio to a pergola on either side of the garden. Arrange benches or chairs beneath the per-

Left: Wild Quinine, Prairie Blazing Star, Purple Coneflower, and Prairie Baby's Breath bloom in the side gardens in this design.

Right: Pale Purple Coneflower makes a stunning focal point in June through mid-July.

A comfortable chair beneath a rose-clad arbor is another marvelous spot for abandoning yourself to marvelous dreams....

—**Stephen Lacey,** *The Startling Jungle*

Left: Gold Flame Honeysuckle climbs the pillars of the pergola.

Right: Alabaster Wild Quinine and Foxglove Beard Tongue shimmer to the side gardens in summer.

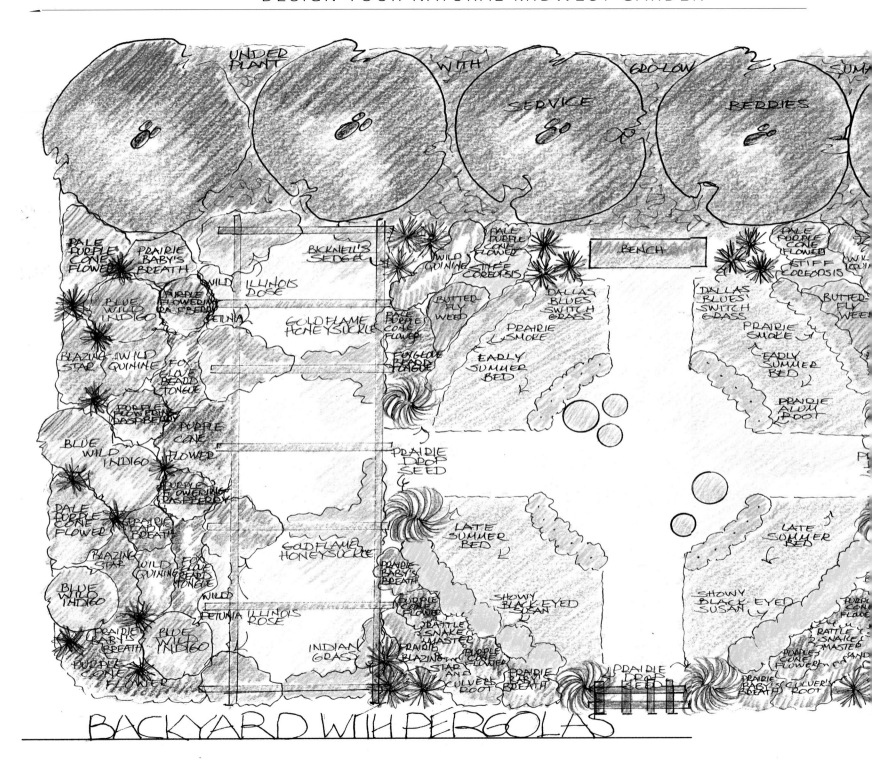

BACKYARD WITH PERGOLAS

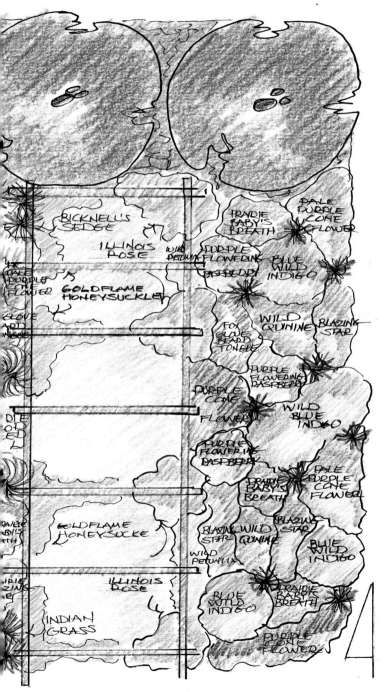

golas, a comfortable shady place from which to view the gardens. The spectacular Illinois Rose climbs the pillars on the outside edge of the pergola, while 'Gold Flame' Honeysuckle grows up the inside.

Blue Wild Indigo and the notable Bicknell's Sedge begin to bloom in May, joined by gleaming white Foxglove Beard Tongue and mauve Pale Purple Coneflower in June. Wild Quinine begins its summer-long, June through August flowering The fuchsia silk flowers of Purple Flowering Raspberry open mid-June and last until mid-July, while Illinois Rose blooms from the end of June through the beginning of July. Purple Coneflower, Prairie Blazing Star, and Prairie Baby's Breath carry on in July and August. ❧

DESIGN FOR A WHITE GARDEN BETWEEN TWO DECKS
Partial Shade, Medium to Moist Soil

MY FORMER WHITE GARDEN came about quite by accident. Some time ago, I had planted the white-barked 'Whitespire Senior' Gray Birch near the wooden walkway that connected the family room and bedroom decks. PJM Rhododendrons grew and bloomed close to the foundation. A little fountain bubbled up next to the walkway surrounded by periwinkle. I had planted a few pale yellow 'Hyperion' daylilies and white 'Deutschland' *Astilbe* as accents; green and white *Hosta undulata* grew nearby (so far, all exotic plants). Then a few clumps of Meadow Anemone appeared within the periwinkle, having emigrated from a garden some distance away. Within a season, the Meadow Anemone had completely overtaken the periwinkle, much to my delight. And then the white astilbe bloomed and I couldn't help but notice I had the beginning of a "white garden."

Many designers create "moon gardens" that feature white flowers (preferably fragrant, as well) to show off at night. The white garden at Sissinghurst is Vita Sackville-West's most famous garden, about what she says: " ... the grey, green, white, silver garden which looks so cool on a summer evening." (V. Sackville-West, *The Illustrated Garden Book*, A New Anthology by Robin Lane Fox) If you more often than not view your garden in the evening when the light is dimming, or if the garden is in shade, white flowers are more visible than any other color.

I replaced the rhododendrons with 'Annabelle' Hydrangea, a cultivar of the native Smooth Hydrangea to continue the white and green color scheme. The cool white "snowball" flowers are refreshing on a summer's day, sparkling even in deep shade.

I gave away the hosta, daylilies, and astilbe and then proceeded to fill in the partly shady area with white-flowering native plants. I replaced the hosta with Prairie Alum Root, which is a similar size and shape. Hosta deteriorates in hot weather, its leaves shredded by slugs, but the Prairie Alum Root never flags—its robust clump of leaves remains bright green all summer. It edges the wooden walk on both sides between the decks.

Clumps of the striking Northern Sea Oats (*Uniola latifolium*) or Spike Grass rise up along the back and one side of the fountain. The horizontal, yellow-green leaves resemble bamboo, a distinctive and attractive feature in itself; then in mid-July, large, flat seeds that resemble oats hang from thread-like pedicels underneath the arching stems. Green at first, they become tawny in late summer. Plant it in full or partial shade in moist soil—it is especially striking when grown next to water. In addition, it is stunning when grown in a pot, and it dries beautifully for indoor arrangements. It readily seeds itself —in no time you will have babies to increase your own plantings or to give away. Rare in the Chicago region, in the wild it is found in shaded floodplains. It is sometimes listed in catalogues as Chasmanthium latifolia.

Tall wands of white bottlebrush flowers of Black Cohosh grow to 6' from large divided leaves in back of the Northern Sea Oats. The spectacular Spikenard is placed in the back corner next to the bedroom deck; its lacy, umbellose white flower clusters create a stunning focal point. Goat's Beard will also work in this situation, with its magnificent creamy feathery plumes, up to a foot long, in bloom from early to mid-June.

Some day I should like to plant a garden to the night, to be frequented only at dim twilight, by moonlight, or when there is no light save the faint luminousness of white flowers. There should be somber evergreens for mystery, an ever-playing fountain to break the tenseness, a pool for the moon's quaint artistry, and a seat. And nearly all the flowers should be white and sweet. —Louise Beebe Wilder, *Color in My Garden*

'Annabelle' Hydrangea and Northern Sea Oats make an eye-catching combination in shade.

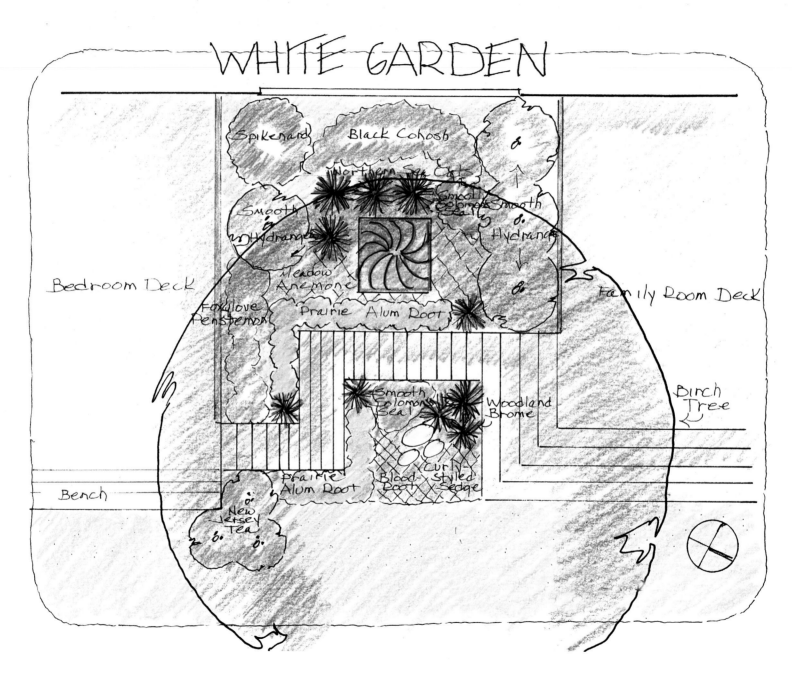

WHITE GARDEN

Spikenard

Black Cohosh

Northern Sea Oats

Smooth Solomon's Seal

Smooth

Smooth Hydrangea

Smooth Hydrangea

Meadow Anemone

Bedroom Deck

Foxglove Penstemon

Prairie Alum Root

Family Room Deck

Smooth Solomon's Seal

Woodland Brome

Birch Tree

Prairie Alum Root

Blood Root

Curly-styled Sedge

Bench

New Jersey Tea

During the American Revolution, the colonists made tea from the leaves of New Jersey Tea, therefore the common name. To make tea, pick the leaves when the plant is in full bloom. Dry and store in an airtight container.

—Shirley Shirley, *Restoring the Tallgrass Prairie*

A row of gleaming white spikes of 'Husker Red' Foxglove Beardtongue (*Penstemon digitalis*) marches alongside the bedroom deck. The bright white, waxy trumpets are arranged in tiers around smooth, straight, 2′ to 3′ stems. The species, frequently seen in older gardens, has thick, dark green, waxy, opposite leaves, while 'Husker Red', a new cultivar, mentioned above, has burgundy leaves and stems. 'Husker Red' was named Perennial Plant of the Year in 1996, and therefore it has been widely promoted and widely available. Situate it in partial or full sun in home gardens and landscaping. (Don't plant the species next to an outdoor sitting area or along pathways—in late summer and fall the seedpods have an unpleasant, pungent odor.)

Three clumps of New Jersey Tea (*Ceanothus americanus*) curl around the outside corner of the bedroom deck. The lime-green, quilted, ovate leaves form a beautiful backdrop for the long-stalked clusters of tiny white blossoms that bloom in June and July. The flowers are attractive to many species of bees and butterflies, as well as other insects and hummingbirds. Unfortunately, rabbits and deer are also attracted by the subtle scent of the leaves and can devour the whole plant. One of the few shrubs that grow on the prairie, it has a huge, branched rootstock—early farmers called it "rupture root." Like legumes, the roots have the ability to fix nitrogen. It is found in dry or mesic prairies, sandy Black Oak savannas, and woodland edges.

Smooth Solomon's Seal popped up within the Meadow Anemone, its arched stems repeating the curve of the Northern

The waxy trumpets of 'Husker Red' Foxglove Beardtounge make and appealing addition to a white-flower garden.

Sea Oats. The arched foliage of the daylilies was replaced with the arched stems of Woodland Brome next to the birch tree trunks. The remaining area was filled in with Curly-styled Sedge, Bloodroot, Dutchman's Breeches, and Great White Trillium.

Our green and white garden will look cool and refreshing even on 90° summer days. It will be enchanting at dusk and beyond—even more so with the twinkling of fireflies that begins around the first of July. Add lots of white candles in glass votives, light up the fountain, put low-voltage lighting along the boardwalk, and perhaps even up light the tree. ∾

ATTRACTING BUTTERFLIES

EVERYONE RECOGNIZES the showy orange and black monarch butterfly, but we don't pay much notice to the rest of the butterfly nation, to our loss. There are dozens of species of butterflies, large and small, in an array of colors to delight us. Planting a "butterfly garden" to attract various butterflies will enhance our lives immeasurably.

Most prairie forbs are pollinated by butterflies, so every prairie garden will attract butterflies to its bountiful nectar supplies. But you can augment your yard or garden to be even more appealing to butterflies. An area with full sun, especially between 10:00 a.m. and 3:00 p.m., the hours of peak butterfly activity, with shelter from the wind, is the most favored location. Since butterflies use their wings as solar panels, their body temperature must be above 80° for optimum flight—providing flat stones in the sun for basking will benefit them. They also appreciate a shallow puddle or even a low, damp, or muddy area for drinking and for congregating.

Butterflies are most abundant from mid-June through mid-September. It is important to have butterfly-attracting flowers in bloom all season that will provide a continuous supply of nectar. Butterflies have definite color preferences, purple being the overwhelming favorite, followed by pink, then yellow, and finally white.

Milkweeds of all kinds are favored not only by monarchs, but by a wider variety of butterfly species than any other plant. While the Common Milkweed is too aggressive for use in home gardens, its look-alike cousin, Prairie Milkweed (*Asclepias sullivantii*), is a high-quality denizen of moist to wet prairies. The vibrant tangerine Butterfly Weed is the showiest of the *Asclepias* genus, attracting butterflies in June and July in dry prairies and sandy Black Oak savannas. Yet another Asclepias, the white-flowered Whorled Milkweed (*Asclepias verticillata*), is common in dry pastures, along roadsides, and on dry slopes. Very pretty, it's seldom noticed by us, but monarchs find it attractive.

Pale Purple and Purple Coneflowers attract many species of butterfly, particularly Red Admiral, Painted Lady, Otto Skipper, and Great Spangled Fritillary.

All species of phlox appeal to butterflies, especially monarchs, swallowtails, and sulfurs. Prairie Phlox and Marsh Phlox bloom in spring and early summer; the July-August garden features Garden and Meadow Phlox. Garden Phlox (*Phlox paniculata*) is indigenous to the southeastern United States, but it is also found in the Midwest in savanna and woodland. It thrives in sunny areas, as well. Meadow Phlox or Wild Sweet William (*Phlox maculatum*) is encountered in wetter areas, but it will also thrive in good garden soil. Its flower clusters are conical in shape, while those of Garden Phlox form a rounded dome. Unlike Garden Phlox, Meadow Phlox is highly resistant to mildew.

Profuse, mauve, vanilla-scented, fringed flower clusters bloom at the top of 3′ to 5′ erect stems of the striking Joe Pye Weeds in late summer and early fall. They attract hoards of butterflies such as tiger swallowtails, painted ladies, monarchs, and Great Spangled Fritillaries. Other butterfly favorites in the purple, lavender, violet, and rosy palette are the fragrant Wild Bergamot and all kinds of blazing stars.

Every sort of yellow daisy, such as coreopsis, black-eyed Susan's, sunflowers, rosin weeds, and especially goldenrods appeal to butterflies, particularly swallowtails, sulfurs, monarchs, painted ladies, red admirals, and viceroys. One August I

Left: Monarch butterfly nectaring on New England Aster.

Page 54: Purple Joe Pye Weed, Culver's Root, Yellow Coneflower, and Purple Coneflower bloom along the west side of my house in late July.

Above left:Tiny Eastern Tailed Blue on the Purple Joe Pye Weed in my savanna garden.

Below left: Smooth Blue Aster and Painted Lady.

Right: Showy Goldenrod is attractive to Red Admirals.

had a "pet" tiger swallowtail that visited my prairie garden almost every day. The first time I saw it, it lingered for hours sipping nectar from my Cup Plants. A few days later, I saw it on the Purple Joe Pye Weed, the next time, on the Royal Catchfly. It is not uncommon for a tiger swallowtail to hang around-when it finds a garden it likes, it will return again and again, always nectaring on tall plants, according to Doug Taron, curator of biology at the Peggy Notebaert Nature Museum of the Chicago Academy of Sciences and leader of the Butterfly Monitoring Project of the Volunteer Stewardship Network.

Asters in their full range of purple, lavender, violet, and white, such as Sky-blue, Smooth Blue, Aromatic, Silky, Heath, and especially New England Aster round out the list of plants that attract butterflies. Smooth Blue Aster (*Aster laevis*) is lavender, not blue, but it does have smooth leaves and stems. Its dark-green leaves clasp the stiff stems, a characteristic that makes this plant easy to identify. It grows 1′ to 4′ tall in a narrow, upright fashion, but soon spills over nearby plants in fluffy billows of intense lavender-blue. This aster also grows in the partial shade of savannas.

The most colorful and best known of the species asters is the New England Aster (*Aster novae-angliae*) with intense purple flowers that bloom from early September to the end of October. Adaptable, it grows in prairies, wetlands, and ditches, and along roadsides and railroad tracks. Asters are especially appealing to painted ladies, red admirals, monarchs, vice-roys, the tiny orange and black Pearly Crescentspot, and the yellow sulfurs.

Clouds of painted ladies descended upon my garden in mid-September, 2003, and hung around until mid-October. They first began to nectar on Stiff Goldenrod, then Showy Goldenrod, then all the purple and blue asters.

Above: Tiger Swallowtail on Spotted Joe Pye Weed.

Below: Tiger Swallowtail on Purple Joe Pye Weed. Note the flower head of Spotted Joe Pye Weed is flat, while that of the Purple Joe Pye Weed is dome-shaped.

Note how Tiger Swallowtail blends into the daisy flowers of Cup Plant.

BUTTERFLY LARVAE

Providing nectar flowers for the butterflies is only half the story—you must also provide food for the less than attractive caterpillars and be willing to look the other way when they munch through your prize Butterfly Weeds.

I've mentioned, from time to time, various plants that are attractive to different caterpillars. Everyone knows the caterpillars of monarchs eat only milkweeds. Legumes such as clovers, vetches, tick trefoils, and wild indigos attract the caterpillars of sulfurs, painted ladies, gray hairstreaks, Eastern-tailed Blues, and Silver-spotted Skippers.

The larvae of Spring Azures feed on New Jersey Tea; Marine Blues prefer Lead Plant; the caterpillars of Delaware Skippers, Little Wood Satyrs, Common Wood Nymphs are attracted to grasses such as Little Bluestem, Switch Grass, and Indian Grass.

Plants of the parsley family such as Golden Alexanders, Heart-leaved Meadow Parsnip, Great Angelica, Rattlesnake Master, and the alien Queen Anne's Lace appeal only to Black Swallowtails; in turn, Black Swallowtails only feed on members of the parsley family or umbellifers.

Situate your garden near or around a terrace or gazebo or a large front porch that lets you sit and observe the flitting not only of butterflies, but also of bees and other insects. Hummingbirds and Gold Finches will also be attracted to the flowers in profusion. ∾

I always grow a pot of parsley near my back door. One day, in late summer, I went outside to cut some herbs for a salad and noticed two small caterpillars on the parsley. I snipped carefully around them; then a few days later I again went outside for more parsley and found two huge caterpillars—they reminded me of Eric Karle's The Very Hungry Caterpillar, a story that I used to read to my grandchildren. Only the stems of the parsley remained—all the leaves had been eaten! This was a small sacrifice to make for the prospect of more Black Swallowtail butterflies. (The parsley grew new leaves within a few weeks.)

The brilliant orange Monarch butterfly is a striking contrast to the royal purple of New England Aster.

DESIGN FOR A SUNNY BUTTERFLY GARDEN
Sun, Medium to Dry-Medium Soil

THIS GARDEN IS ENTERED through a honeysuckle-covered arbor. The flagstone walk curves around a central island and then opens up to an arbor-covered bench. The round lawn is surrounded by a border of plants that particularly appeal to butterflies, with a color scheme of purple, lavender-blue, rose-purple, and golden yellow.

Two tall Hackberry shelter the far corners of the garden and provide light shade for the lofty Purple Joe Pye Weed and Pale-leaved Sunflower More tall prairie forbs and grasses make up the back row of the garden; successive rows cascade down like stair steps with ever-lower growing plants. The flagstone walk may be planted with the small, limestone-loving plants mentioned in the section on Terrace Gardens. A small mud puddle is contained within the center circle garden along with New Jersey Tea, bearing clusters of fluffy white blossoms, vibrant purple-flowered Lead Plant, and brilliant orange Butterfly Weed. Three clumps of Little Bluestem grow on the raised limestone ledge. If your soil is sandy, plant a Buffalo Grass lawn and dot it with Shooting Star and Common Cinquefoil. ✿

The shaggy lavender Wild Bergamot (*Monarda fistulosa*) is attractive to both butterflies and hummingbirds.

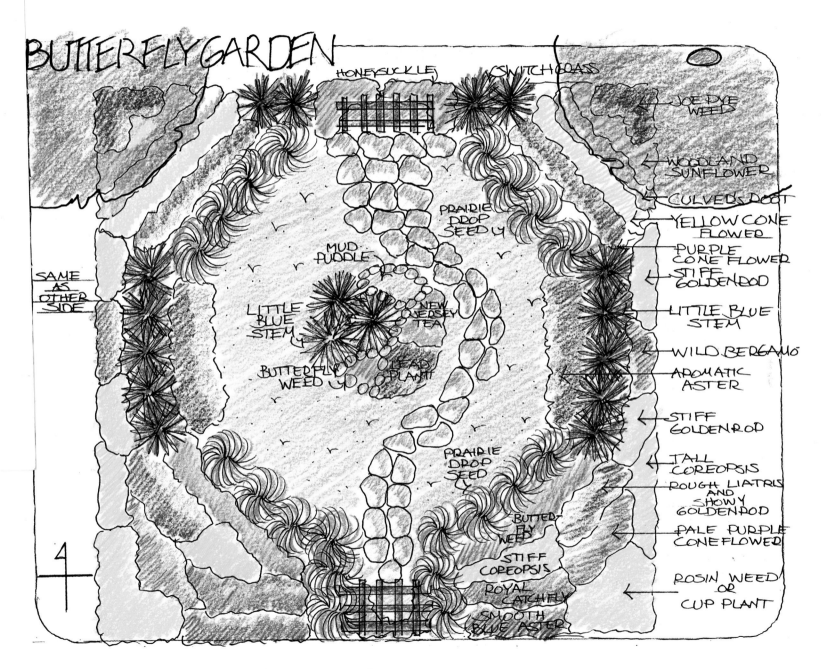

BUTTERFLY GARDEN

HONEYSUCKLE

SWITCHGRASS

JOE PYE WEED

WOODLAND SUNFLOWER

CULVERS ROOT

YELLOW CONE FLOWER

PURPLE CONE FLOWER

STIFF GOLDENROD

LITTLE BLUE STEM

WILD BERGAMO

AROMATIC ASTER

STIFF GOLDENROD

TALL COREOPSIS

ROUGH LIATRIS AND SHOWY GOLDENROD

PALE PURPLE CONEFLOWER

ROSIN WEED OR CUP PLANT

PRAIRIE DROP SEED

MUD PUDDLE

LITTLE BLUE STEM

NEW JERSEY TEA

BUTTERFLY WEED

LEAD PLANT

PRAIRIE DROP SEED

BUTTER FLY WEED

STIFF COREOPSIS

ROYAL CATCHFLY

SMOOTH BLUE ASTER

SAME AS OTHER SIDE

4

ATTRACTING HUMMINGBIRDS

NODDING RED AND YELLOW BELLS of the graceful Wild Columbine (*Aquilegia canadensis*) dance on long stalks above delicate, light green, lacy foliage. Long yellow stamens protrude from the inner circle of matching petals; long red spurs stream from the outer ring of red sepals, giving it an airy grace. It seeds itself with wild abandon; anyone who has planted one now has dozens, but its prolificacy doesn't make it any less beautiful. It comes up where one might not have thought to plant it, which often is the perfect place While it spreads aggressively in cultivated home gardens, it is uncommon in the wild. Its natural habitat is in shady woods or on limestone ledges.

In addition to its own loveliness, it is wildly attractive to Ruby-throated Hummingbirds. Hummingbirds are our tiniest birds—only 3¹/₂″ long. They are iridescent green above; the male has a brilliant ruby throat, while the female is white below. They frequent gardens and orchards in order to satisfy their taste for sweets found in flower nectar (it takes nectar from 1,000 flowers a day to satisfy a hummingbird's need for carbohydrates). Their long, hollow, needlelike bill inserts readily into tubular or trumpet-shaped flowers; for unknown reasons, the tiny birds prefer red, orange, or yellow blossoms. By planting a succession of red, orange, or yellow tubular or trumpet-shaped flowers, you will have visiting Ruby-throated Hummingbirds all summer long from their arrival in mid-April from Central America until their departure in mid-September.

Begin with the American Columbine, just discussed. Follow with Prairie Alum Root, a relative of the familiar Coral

Left: The trumpets of Foxglove Beardtongue and the orange hue of Butterfly Weed attract hummingbirds.

The red trumpet-shaped blossoms of the 'Dropmore Scarlet' Honeysuckle vine that drapes over a stone wall at the Chicago Botanic Garden are particularly appealing to hummingbirds.

Bells, with tiny, greenish bells at the top of tall stems in May and June. Continue with Foxglove Beard Tongue with white, waxy tube flowers that bloom in May and June and orange, flat-topped Butterfly Weed for June and July. Then add Wild Petunia with lavender-blue trumpets, Wild Bergamot with shaggy, tubular, lavender flowers, and especially Royal Catchfly with tiny, red, star-shaped tube flowers, all good choices for July and August bloom.

The shaggy, lavender, mopheads of Wild Bergamot (*Monarda fistulosa*) bloom at the top of 3' to 4' square stems in July and into August. The blossoms are redolent of mint—the fragrant lance- or arrow-shaped leaves may be dried and used for tea (its taste is reminiscent of Earl Grey tea, which contains natural oil of bergamot). It is widespread in disturbed dry prairie remnants, in pastures, along railroad tracks, and in open savannas. It will sometimes succumb in wet winters.

I've never seen Royal Catchfly (*Silene regia*) in the wild—it is rare in the Chicago area. It is more often found in the dry and mesic prairies and open oak savannas in the southern Midwestern region, although it is uncommon there, as well. Striking scarlet, star-shaped flowers bloom on the top half of 3'- to 4'-tall, unbranched stems from mid-July until almost the end of August. It adds punch to any color scheme. The blossoms emerge from long, tubular, pale-green, sticky, hairy, ribbed calyces that trap insects: therefore, the common name, "Catchfly." Even though it is scarce in the wild, it is easily found in commerce.

Hummingbirds, like butterflies, are also attracted to phloxes of all kinds. All the blazing stars with tall spikes of showy, rose-purple, feathery blossoms in July and August are

The red trumpet flowers of Royal Catchfly are a magnet to hummingbirds.

The tubular blossoms of Obedient Plant also appeal to hummingbirds.

Columbines, with their poised blossoms and streaming spurs, are charmingly buoyant in effect. They are the most enchanting of flowers. Even the debonair little red-and-yellow native sort that we are so glad to meet upon our April walks, rollicking over a great brooding rock, is fit to be brought into the garden to shine among the best. —**Louise Beebe Wilder,** *Color in My Garden*

also attractive to hummingbirds.

Hummingbirds also frequent woodland streams, where more of their favorite flowers occur. The spectacular Cardinal Flower (*Lobelia cardinalis*) with scarlet trumpets on 2′ to 4′ spikes in July and August is especially favored. Another favorite found in the same situation is Showy Obedient Plant (*Physostegia virginiana, var. speciosa*) with rose-lavender, lipped tube-flowers that bloom on the 1′ to 3′ spikes from mid-August until mid- September.

The spotted orange trumpets of the annual Orange Jewelweed or Spotted Touch-me-not also attract hummingbirds. A common inhabitant of shaded floodplains, fens, sunny marshes, and mesic woods, it blooms from early July until early October. Its pale yellow cousin, Yellow Jewelweed or Pale Touch-me-not, also grows in moist shady areas, particularly around limestone.

One of the most often mentioned attractants for hummingbirds is the Trumpet Creeper (*Campsis radicans*), a vine with large orange or golden trumpets, native to the south of us. But beware—the name is a misnomer. It doesn't creep; it gallops, engulfing and strangling everything in sight. It suckers from its rootstock, which makes it extremely difficult to eradicate or even control.

Better choices are the Yellow Honeysuckle and the Red Honeysuckle. Whorls of large, pale-yellow, trumpet flowers of Yellow Honeysuckle (*Lonicera prolifera*) bloom in June at the end of the stem that pierces the circle leaf like a Victorian bouquet poking through a doily. The blossoms are followed later in the summer by equally attractive red berries that are relished by birds. The Red or Limber Honeysuckle (*Lonicera dioica*) is similar, but with reddish-yellow flowers that bloom in May

and June. The Yellow Honeysuckle is available in commerce, but I have not seen the Red.

If these prove hard to find, the hybrid Gold Flame Honeysuckle and the cultivated 'Dropmore Scarlet' Honeysuckle are both readily available in garden centers and nurseries and are especially attractive to hummingbirds.

These flowers need not be grouped in a "Hummingbird Garden"—plant them anywhere their cultural conditions are met. But place them in view of windows or terraces where the tiny birds that feed on them can be viewed with ease for many moments of delight. ❧

Wild Columbine is the favorite nectar source of hummingbirds.

PRIVACY

MANY HOMEOWNERS in my neighborhood enclose their side yards or backyards with a six-foot-high, solid board fence for privacy reasons. But if others can't see in, no one can see out either—it strikes me as dreadfully confining. Unless one wants to cavort naked in one's backyard, a much better solution is to plant tall forbs and grasses that are beautiful in their own right and provide, not a solid barrier, but a delightful pierced curtain through which light, images, and breezes pass.

My side yard is only 20′ wide—a fence or shrubbery border would have made the space seem smaller, even claustrophobic. In very early spring, after a burn, the area is exposed to the sidewalk and the street, but as the weather warms the greenery grows quickly through the year to enclose the area. The seating spot not only affords privacy, but also an ever-changing view of colorful flowers and butterflies and a gentle, caressing breeze.

Shooting Stars, Heart-leaved Meadow Parsnip, and Bicknell's Sedge provide charm in May, followed by the spectacular Pale Purple Coneflower in June. The foliage becomes thicker and the plants taller in July as Rosin Weed and Royal Catchfly come into bloom. Finally, the tallgrasses, asters, and goldenrods reach their zenith in September, further enclosing the sitting area. ❧

Left: Shooting Star, Heart-leaved Meadow Parsnip, and various sedges define the edge of this seating area in spring.

Right: Purple Coneflower and Red Switch Grass give privacy in late summer.

The tall—up to 4'—
Pale Purple Coneflower
provides a pierced curtain
to obscure seating area
in June.

DESIGN FOR A PRIVATE SIDE YARD

MY CLIENT'S KITCHEN WINDOW overlooked a small side yard that was adjacent to an unsightly alley that she wanted screened. I had the existing border of Cranberry Cotoneaster removed and, following her color scheme of purples, fuchsias, and reds, I planted Red Switch Grass, Joe Pye Weed, Prairie Blazing Star, and Purple Coneflower along the side of the alley. The small lawn area was then encircled with more native plants using the same delightful color combination plus shimmering white. A terrace could take the place of the lawn; chairs and an umbrella table could be placed on either the lawn or a terrace for a private retreat. ∾

Showy Black-eyed Susan, Royal Catchfly, and various grasses give privacy in July.

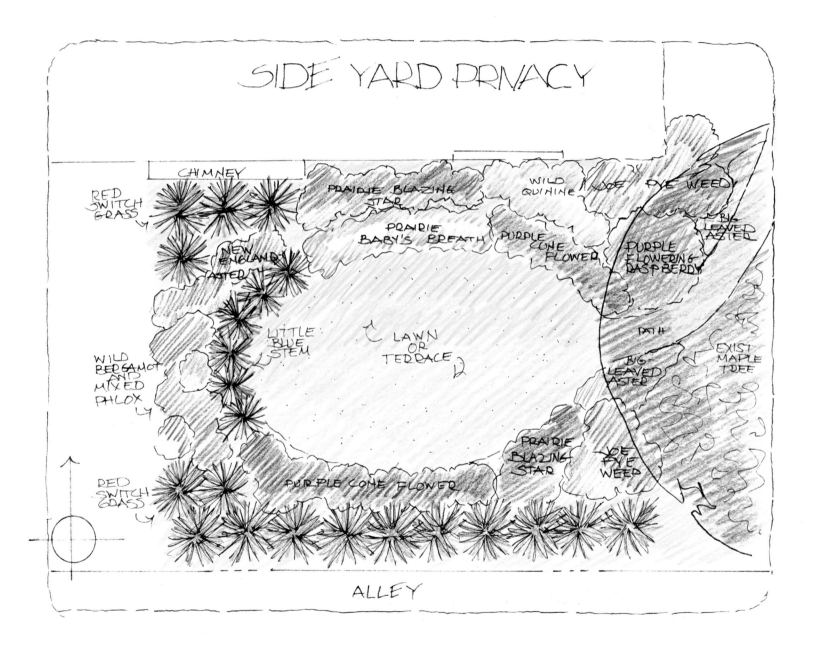

SIDE YARD PRIVACY

CHIMNEY

RED SWITCH GRASS

PRAIRIE BLAZING STAR

WILD QUININE

JOE PYE WEED

PRAIRIE BABY'S BREATH

PURPLE CONE FLOWER

BIG LEAVED ASTER

PURPLE FLOWERING RASPBERRY

NEW ENGLAND ASTER

LITTLE BLUE STEM

LAWN OR TERRACE

PATH

BIG LEAVED ASTER

EXIST MAPLE TREE

WILD BERGAMOT AND MIXED PHLOX

PRAIRIE BLAZING STAR

JOE PYE WEED

RED SWITCH GRASS

PURPLE CONE FLOWER

ALLEY

DAISY GARDENS

"DAISY GARDENS," featuring only plants of the *Compositae,* or as it is now called, the *Asteraceae* or daisy family, are popular in England, but are unheard of here, except along railroad tracks. Not quite true—there is such a garden at Chicago Botanic Garden, a Daisy Garden within an English garden. Daisy beds surround the perimeter of a sunny, crushed stone terrace, and daisies fill the beds around the center obelisk.

The daisy family includes all those flowers that have large daisy blossoms, such as asters, ragworts, sunflowers, black-eyed Susan's, coneflowers, blanket flowers, coreopsis, rosin weeds, False Sunflower, False Aster, and Sneezeweed, as well as flowers that have tiny daisies arranged closely together that form different shapes, such as goldenrods and Wild Quinine. There are some that have only disc flowers, such as Indian Plantain, blazing stars, ironweeds, eupatorium, and thistles. There are a few with only ray flowers such as Cynthia, dandelion, sow thistles, and hawkweeds. With such a large palette, there are ample flowers to choose from to make an all "daisy" garden.

Nearly 10% of the flowering plant species that grow in the Midwest are members of the daisy family (Asteracae) and yellow daisies in particular are ubiquitous in the summer and fall landscape.

—Thomas M. Antonio and Susanne Masi,
The Sunflower Family in the Upper Midwest

Left: Yellow Coneflower, Purple Coneflower, and Wild Bergamot bloom in prairie border in July.

Right: False Sunflower and Wild Quinine for a sunny composition in July and August.

The daisy, in some form or other, is as characteristic of tall prairie as are grass and grasshoppers.
—**John Madson,** ***Where the Sky Began: Land of the Tallgrass Prairie***

Daisy Garden within the English Garden at the Chicago Botanic Garden.

Tall Cup Plants seem to tower above roofline.

YELLOW DAISIES

Radiant yellow daisies dominate July–August gardens. The first to bloom is the common Black-eyed Susan (*Rudbeckia hirta*), a self-sowing annual or biennial. The golden-yellow daisy with a dark-brown center blooms at the top of 2′ to 3′ stiff, hairy stems clothed with coarsely hairy leaves. It opens in June and continues blooming sporadically through October.

Long, notably reflexed, yellow petals surround a tall prominent cone of the Yellow Coneflower (*Ratibida pinnata*), in bloom from early July to mid-August. The cone is pale golden brown at first, becoming deep brown, and then gray as the seeds drop (another name for this plant is Gray-headed Coneflower). It grows 3′ to 5′ tall in a garden situation. It is common along railroad tracks and in dry prairies, frequently in the company of Wild Bergamot, a good combination for the home garden, as well.

The cheerful, brilliantly colored orange-yellow daisies of False Sunflower (*Heliopsis helianthoides*) bloom from late June through August. Large, opposite, long-stalked triangular leaves appear on 3′ to 4′ smooth stems that form a loosely branched clump. It is abundant in disturbed prairies, frequently in the company of Wild Bergamot and Yellow Coneflower. It is also found along woodland borders and in savanna openings. Adaptable in the home landscape, it grows in sun or partial shade. It is an aggressive seeder, so plant it with other strong plants such as the above, or with Purple Coneflower. It is not drought-tolerant—during hot summers with little rainfall, it will stop blooming and wilt significantly.

While the Stiff Coreopsis fades in early July, Tall Coreopsis (*Coreopsis tripteris*) blooms from late July through Aug-

ust. The golden-rayed, brown-centered daisies grow in branched clusters at the top of 6′- to 7′-tall, smooth, wandlike stems. The distinctive leaves are divided into three lance-shaped leaflets. It's found in prairies and thin, sandy woods.

We mentioned the Showy Black-eyed Susan earlier-it dominates gardens from mid-July to mid-September.

What a thousand acres of Silphiums looked like when they tickled the bellies of the buffalo is a question never again to be answered, and perhaps not even asked.
—Aldo Leopold, *A Sand County Almanac*

ROSIN WEEDS

All the blossoms of various members of the genus *Silphium* are canary yellow all over. (Collectively, the genus *Silphium* is called Rosin Weed because of the resin produced along the stems and on the flower stalks of all the species.)

Rosin Weed (*Silphium integrifolium*) grows 2′ to 5′ tall in the prairie; in my garden it is over my head. (If you want a smaller plant, cut the stems back hard at the end of May.) Clusters of large, 3″ diameter, canary-yellow daisies bloom at the top of the stems in July and August. The rough, sandpapery, stalkless leaves are arranged in pairs along the length of the stiff stem.

The huge, triangular, opposite leaves of the Cup Plant or Indian Cup (*Silphium perfoliatum*) encircle the thick, square stem to form a cup that holds rainwater. These little reservoirs provide water for birds, butterflies, dragonflies, and other insects. Clusters of large, 2″- to 4″-wide, lemon-yellow daisy flowers bloom in the upper part of 3′- to 8′-tall stems from mid-July through August. This plant is common on floodplains near streams and in fens; it will also grow in ordinary soil in home gardens. My Cup Plants appeared spontaneously in my prairie garden among clumps of Switch Grass. An aggressive seeder, it pops up in bare spots throughout my sunny gardens.

The 3″ to 4″ golden blossoms of the Compass Plant (*Silphium laciniatum*) bloom alternately along the top half of its 3′ to 9′ stems from early July through mid- to late August. But its most striking feature is its magnificent, outsized, oak leaf-shaped leaves. They orient themselves in a north–south position, thus providing an accurate compass for native tribes and early pioneers.

The enormous, rough, spade-shaped basal leaves of Prairie Dock (*Silphium terebinthinaceum*) are a dramatic presence in the prairie or prairie garden from early spring through late fall. Hold your hands on both sides of the leaf—it will feel cold no matter how hot the day. In summer, a smooth, leafless, central stalk rises up to 10′; clusters of 2″ golden daisies with greenish centers begin to bloom the last week in July. In autumn, the leaves turn to a gorgeous red-mahogany.

Locate *Silphium* in large beds away from trees, buildings, or other shade. As a rule of thumb, a garden bed should be three times as wide as the tallest plant. Silphium will reach 7′ to 8′, so the garden should be 20′ to 24′ wide. Integrate them with other strong growers such as Big Bluestem, Indian Grass, Smooth Blue and Heath Aster, Yellow Coneflower, Stiff Coreopsis, Prairie

Left: False Sunflower and Wild Bergamot are a pleasing combination in sun or light shade in July and August.

Right: Showy Black-eyed Susan lines both sides of front sidewalk in August.

Baby's Breath, Stiff Goldenrod, Rattlesnake Master, Wild Quinine, Purple Prairie Clover, and Prairie Dropseed.

As the blossoms of all the species of Silphium fade in August and September, their ripe seed heads become a feeding station for goldfinches.

Few grieved when the last buffalo left Wisconsin, and few will grieve when the last Silphium follows him to the lush prairies of the never-never land.

—Aldo Leopold, *A Sand County Almanac*

Left: A taller daisy border of Cup Plant, Rosin Weed, False Sunflower, and Wild Bergamot line the sidewalk along the long west side.

Right: Self-sown Common Black-eyed Susan, Blue Vervain, and Purple Coneflower.

DESIGN FOR A SUNNY ISLAND DAISY GARDEN
Sun, Medium to Well-Drained Soil

THIS IS AN ISLAND BED, cut out of a sunny backyard, featuring colorful members of the daisy family and grasses. The bed can be flat or slightly raised. This garden is made to be viewed from all sides; therefore the tallest plants are placed in the middle. The striking Prairie Dock is planted off-center at one end, while the equally impressive Compass Plant is placed at the other end; they are connected by a row of Indian Grass intermixed with Tall Coreopsis and Cup Plant. (Cup Plant is indigenous to wet areas, but in my experience it grows anywhere.) Rosin Weed, the fourth member of the Silphium family, also grows in the center of the bed next to the Indian Grass.

Tall Pale Purple Coneflower, Prairie Blazing Star, Stiff Goldenrod, and Smooth Blue Aster surround the Silphium and Indian Grass; the next tier consists of Stiff Coreopsis, Yellow Coneflower, Showy Tick Trefoil, Wild Quinine, and Prairie Baby's Breath. Purple Coneflower, Showy Black-eyed Susan, and Purple Prairie Clover fill in next, while Prairie Alum Root, Heath Aster, and Prairie Dropseed, accented with clumps of Rattlesnake Master, grow along the verge.

Rattlesnake Master (*Eryngium yuccifolium*) is like no other plant found in the prairie. Tiny white flowers form prickly globular buttons that grow in clusters at the top of 3′ to 4′ smooth

Left: Prairie Dock makes a stuning accent in the Pocket Prairie Garden at the Chicago Botanic Garden.

Right: Compass Plant tends to lean in a garden situation.

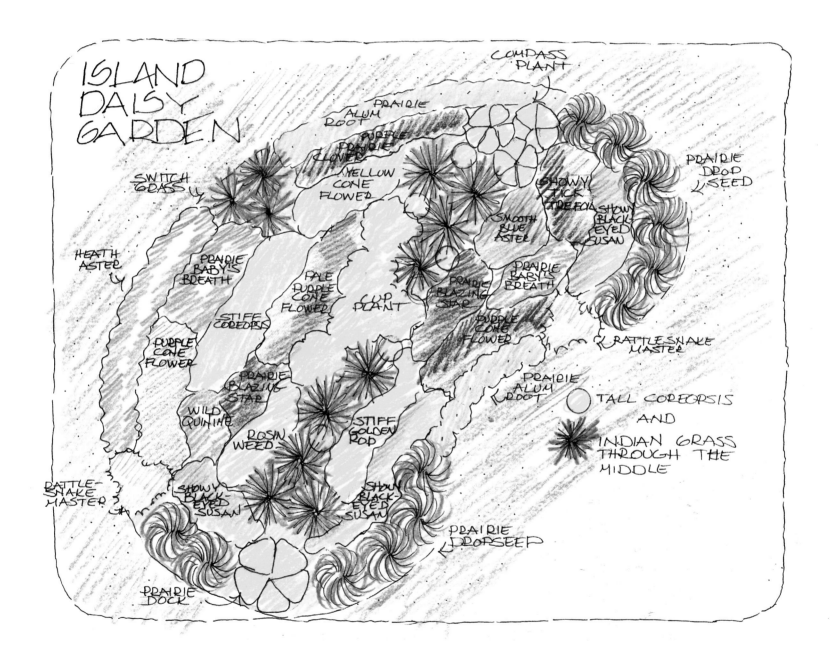

ISLAND DAISY GARDEN

COMPASS PLANT

PRAIRIE ALUM ROOT

PURPLE PRAIRIE CLOVER

YELLOW CONE FLOWER

SWITCH GRASS

SHOWY TICK TREFOIL

SMOOTH BLUE ASTER

SHOWY BLACK-EYED SUSAN

PRAIRIE DROP SEED

HEATH ASTER

PRAIRIE BABY'S BREATH

PALE PURPLE CONE FLOWER

CUP PLANT

PRAIRIE BLAZING STAR

PRAIRIE BABY'S BREATH

STIFF COREOPSIS

PURPLE CONE FLOWER

WILD QUININE

PRAIRIE BLAZING STAR

ROSIN WEED

STIFF GOLDEN ROD

PURPLE CONE FLOWER

PRAIRIE ALUM ROOT

RATTLE SNAKE MASTER

TALL COREOPSIS

AND

INDIAN GRASS THROUGH THE MIDDLE

RATTLE SNAKE MASTER

SHOWY BLACK-EYED SUSAN

SHOWY BLACK-EYED SUSAN

PRAIRIE DROPSEED

PRAIRIE DOCK

Left: The shorter leaves that emerge just below the flower of the Spiderwort resemble a spider—hence the common name.

Right: 'Summer Beauty' Onion is similar to Nodding Wild Onion but is showier and blooms earlier.

prairie, but also along fencerows and railroad tracks.

Shortly, thereafter, a drift of alabaster Wild Quinine begins its long bloom, combining with the Spiderwort and Foxglove Beard Tongue. The silken flowers of Purple Flowering Raspberry bloom throughout June and July. Purple and silver Lead Plant and Purple Prairie Clover begin to bloom at the end of June. Conspicuous, vivid orange stamens decorate the bright purple petals on the 6″ flower spikes of Lead Plant (*Amorpha canescens*) the first week of July. The silky, white hairs that cover the tiny, compound leaves give them a gray or leaden appearance, leading early settlers to believe the plant was an indicator of deposits of lead ore, but that was only a myth. One of the few shrubs native to the prairie, it grows only 2′ to 3′ tall, but its deep roots extend 6′ to 16′ deep into the soil.

In July, rose-purple Prairie Blazing Star and Showy Tick Trefoil, along with amethyst Wild Bergamot, combine with the airy Prairie Baby's Breath. Purple Coneflower, lavender-blue Wild Petunia, silver Rattlesnake Master, white Culver's Root, Prairie Indian Plantain, and the still-blooming Wild Quinine join the grouping to form a glistening, cool combination in July and August.

Elegant candelabras of densely flowered spires of tiny, white tubular blossoms form at the top of the 2′- to 6′-tall Culver's Root (*Veronicastrum virginicum*) in July. Protruding, gold-tipped stamens give the flowers a fringed appearance. A close relative of the garden veronica, *Veronicastrum* means "false veronica." Tiers of five-parted whorled leaves encircle the stems, another attractive feature. Adaptable, it is also found in savannas.

The long-stalked, waxy, parallel-veined basal leaves of Prairie Indian Plantain (*Cacalia plantaginea*) do bear a superfi-

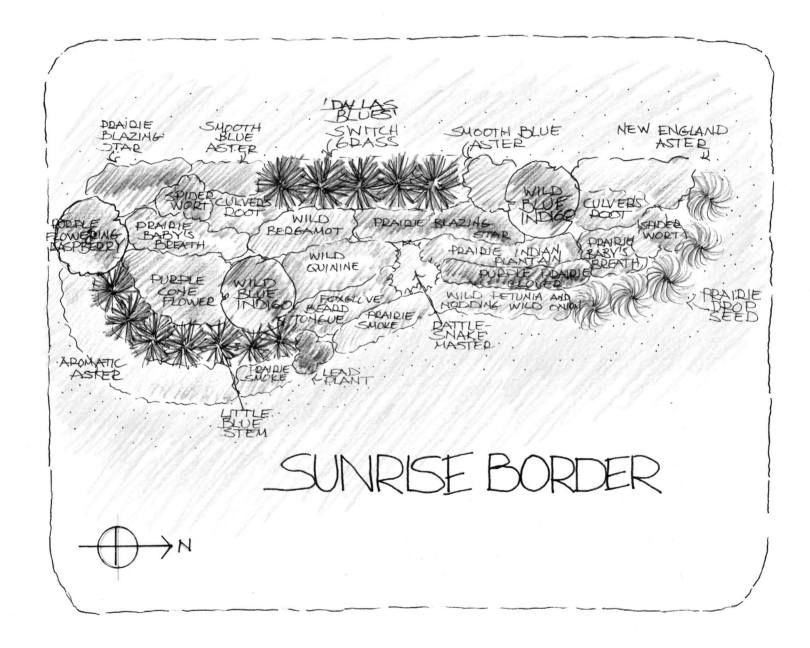

SUNRISE BORDER

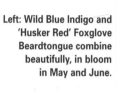

Left: Wild Blue Indigo and 'Husker Red' Foxglove Beardtongue combine beautifully, in bloom in May and June.

Right: Rattlesnake Master as sculpture at Prairie Stone office complex in Hoffman Estates, IL.

cial resemblance to the leaves of the common plantain, a ubiquitous European weed of lawns and compacted paths. But Prairie Indian Plantain is a high-quality denizen of wet and mesic prairies with a distinct elegance. Its tall stems rise up to 3' and end with saucer-sized, flat-topped clusters of tiny, creamy, white disc flowers that bloom in July. Not deeply rooted, it grows from tubers that produce numerous offsets. It prospers from frequent divisions.

The pale-pink spheres of Nodding Wild Onion bloom within the Wild Petunia in August.

'Dallas Blues' Switch Grass and Little Bluestem add their dusty blue-green foliage to the mix. Prairie Dropseed begins its fragrant bloom in August. Lavender-blue Smooth Blue and Aromatic Aster bloom along with the grasses in September. ❧

The Dawn's Awake!
A flash of smoldering flame and fire
Ignites the East. Then higher, higher,
O'er all the sky so gray, forlorn,
The torch of gold is borne.
          —Otto Leland Bohanan, *The Dawn's Awake!*

Left: Close-up of the unusual prickly button blossoms of Rattlesnake Master.

Above right: Lead Plant gets its name from its leaden or silver-colored leaves.

Below: Rosy-purple Prairie Blazing Star and lavender Wild Bergamot in bloom in a July garden.

DESIGN FOR A SUNSET BORDER
Sun

THE SUNSET BORDER was more difficult to put together. While the prairie has a multitude of yellow flowers, orange and red are not much in evidence. So I used a couple of cultivars to get the colors I wanted. Grow this in an open area along your east property line where the long rays of the afternoon sun will shine upon it or along the west property line where it will be backlit by the setting sun. A colorful, showy garden, it will be effective from a distance, as well as close-up.

Three clumps of Indian Grass stand out in the back row —its radiant-yellow anthers are quite spectacular when it blooms in late summer. Arrange Yellow Coneflower, Stiff Goldenrod, New England Aster, Prairie Blazing Star, Royal Catchfly, Shrubby Cinquefoil, and Butterfly Weed around and in front of the Indian Grass in a fiery mixture of gold, purple, scarlet, tangerine, and fuchsia. Brash gold and red 'Indian Summer' Sneezeweed marches along the back row, leading into a fiery mixture of fuchsia Prairie Blazing Star, vivid red 'Gardenview Scarlet' Bee Balm, and brilliant orange Michigan or Turk's Cap Lily (*Lilium michiganense*) at the other end. Spectacular in bloom, the tangerine, backward-curled petals are speckled with deep purple; orange-tipped stamens explode from the center of the nodding blossoms like fireworks in the sky on the Fourth of July. The bulb sends out horizontal rhizomes that produce new plants, which tend to form colonies. It's found in prairies, fens, and moist woodland edges.

Stretch a sinuous ribbon of long-blooming Showy Black-

Left: The prominent cone of the Yellow Coneflower gives it its common name.

Right: The bright golden anthers of Indian Grass are surprisingly showy.

Showy Black-eyed Susan and Purple Coneflower grace the front of this house. A few Rattlesnake Master bloom in the foreground, while Compass Plant blooms in background.

Above left: Native Michigan or Turk's Cap Lily is dazzling in the wild or in the home garden.

Above right: Showy Black-eyed Susan and Purple Coneflower combine in the sidewalk garden.

Bottom left: Prairie Blazing Star and Purple Coneflower add their rosy-purple color to a sunset garden.

Bottom right: Stiff Goldenrod is covered with a flock of Painted Lady butterflies.

eyed Susan through the middle of the border edged with Prairie Drop Seed along the verge, ending at the cluster of the long-blooming Shrubby Potentilla. Shrubby Potentilla (*Potentilla fruiticosa*) is ubiquitous in Midwestern landscapes—it makes a choice foundation plant in a sunny situation because of its affinity for alkaline concrete. Its clusters of bright-yellow flowers bloom from early-June well into November. It grows 3' to 4' tall and around. The Potentilla found in nurseries is derived from a European strain, say Swink and Wilhelm; the native Potentilla fruticosa is available at native plant nurseries.

This garden will begin to bloom in June, and it will be at its floriferous peak in July and August, with the grasses, goldenrods, and asters continuing the color into September and October. The myriad seed heads, pods, and dried stems and leaves will give the garden interest throughout late fall and winter. ❧

Of yellow was the outer Sky
In Yellower Yellow hewn
Till Saffron in Vermilion slid
Whose seam could not be shewn.

—Emily Dickinson

SUNSET BORDER

DESIGN FOR A LONG PRAIRIE BORDER
Sun

WHEN IT COMES TO PRAIRIE GARDENS, bigger is often better. My client lives in a newly built subdivision in a new house with a traditional landscape. But he was a member of The Wild Ones and wanted a prairie garden at the corner of his large backyard.

The Wild Ones was formed in Milwaukee in 1979, an outgrowth of a natural landscaping workshop offered by the Schlitz Audubon Center of Milwaukee in 1977; it has now spread to 39 chapters in eleven states. In 2003, the name was changed to Wild Ones: Native Plants, Natural Landscapes, and a new mission statement was adopted:

Wild Ones: Native Plants, Natural Landscapes promotes environmentally sound landscaping practices to preserve biodiversity through the preservation, restoration, and establishment of native plant communities. Wild Ones is a not-for-profit environmental, educational, and advocacy organization.

This design is based on his garden.

Prairie Smoke and Shooting Star are the first to bloom, followed shortly by Prairie Alum Root. Wild Quinine, Foxglove Beard Tongue, Butterfly Weed, Stiff Coreopsis, Pale Purple Coneflower, White Wild Indigo, and Bicknell's Sedge bloom in June into July. White Wild Indigo (*Baptisia leucantha*) is an elegant plant that deserves to be a focal point of a garden. It stands at the apex of this border with Pale Purple Coneflower in front and Wild Quinine flanking it—all in bloom in June.

Its tall spikes of waxy white pea blossoms bloom from early June into early July on smooth purple-green stems that rise above an open, shrublike plant. The blue-green triparted leaves are attractive all summer long; eye-catching, black seedpods form in late summer and last through the winter. White Wild Indigo is found in dry or mesic prairies and in thin woods.

The beginning of July brings Yellow Coneflower, Purple Coneflower, Rattlesnake Master, Prairie Blazing Star, Wild Bergamot, Rosin Weed, and Compass Plant, while Prairie Dock waits until mid-July to open its yellow daisies.

The *Silphium* lingers into August, joined by all the grasses, while September into October features the purples, blues, and golds of the asters and goldenrod.

THE NEW PRAIRIES

A few corporations located on large suburban campuses have turned to Prairie Style landscaping and discovered that after the first few years of establishment, there is very little cost to maintain the prairie environment. A traditional grass lawn, while relatively inexpensive to install, costs $1500-2500 per acre per year to maintain by regular mowing, fertilization, and the use of herbicides and insecticides; if irrigation is included the costs can go to $4000-$4500 per acre per year. While a prairie initially costs more to install than a lawn, the only expense to maintain an established prairie is annual burn management, at a cost of only $300 per acre per year.

Corporations are persuaded to use native prairie landscaping by economic incentives, but there are other, even more compelling reasons to adopt this concept. The same reasons

The prominent prickly cone of Purple Coneflower resembles the prickly button blossoms of Rattlesnake Master.

given for homeowners to have less lawn apply on a much grander scale to large properties: fuel consumption which releases hydrocarbon emissions into the atmosphere; chemical use of fertilizer, herbicides, and pesticides that is harmful to wildlife and pollutes surface water and groundwater; and irrigation that depletes groundwater supplies. Ultimately, "water management, that of preventing surface water from becoming storm water is the most critical factor to address," declares Jim Patchett, president of Conservation Design Forum, Inc., a leading practitioner of corporate prairie design.

State Departments of Transportation also have adopted native plant landscaping along state highway verges and in traffic islands to replace groundcover monoculture of high upkeep turf grass or exotic Crown Vetch. Native grasses, sedges, and forbs require no mowing-in addition, their deep root systems hold soil in place and promote the absorption of water.

The Audubon Society now certifies golf courses that meet their standards on conservation, habitat protection, water recycling, and safe use of chemicals as Audubon Cooperative Sanctuaries. Again the bottom line is affected: the use of drought-resistant native plants in the rough areas reduces water usage dramatically and the birds that are attracted to the native plants control the mosquitoes that formerly required pesticide applications. In addition, it is aesthetically pleasing. The Audubon Society program began in 1991; there are now more than 300 Audubon-certified golf courses throughout the country, including 27 in Illinois (Star Press.com. East-central Indiana).

Churches with large grounds are replacing lawns with prairie; some are using native plants for foundation landscaping, as well.

Using native plants for large corporate campuses, college

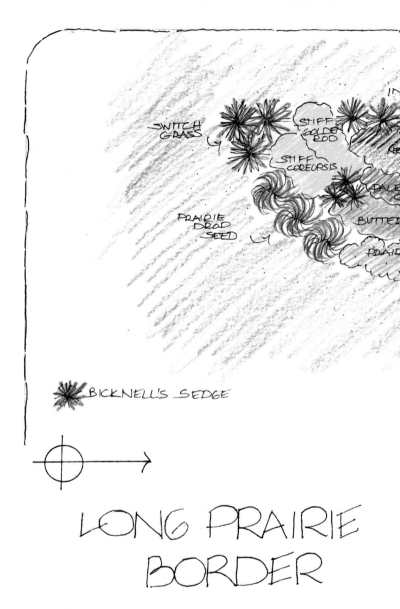

BICKNELL'S SEDGE

LONG PRAIRIE BORDER

campuses, golf courses, state highway verges, and parking lot edges is an idea whose time has come. Environmentalists want legislation passed that will require public money for landscaping to be spent only on indigenous plants. ❧

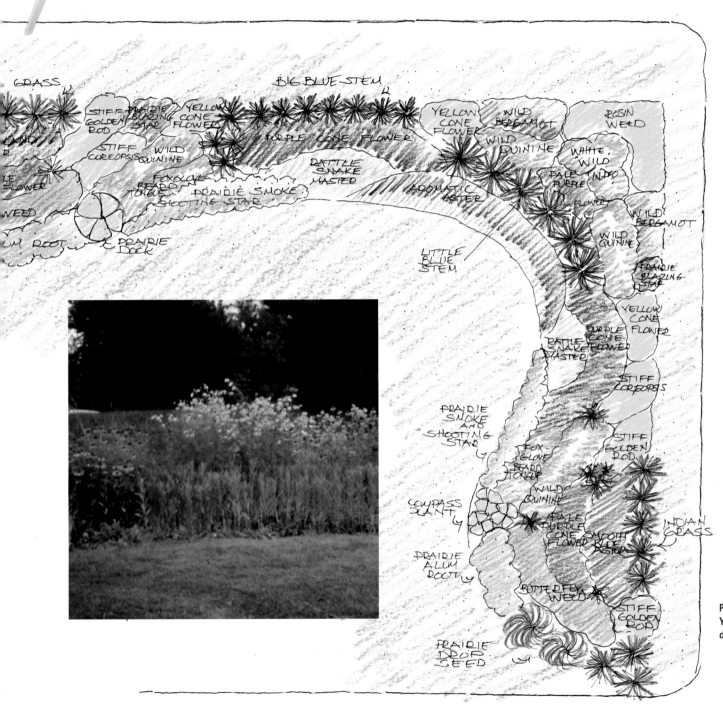

GRASS

BIG BLUE STEM

STIFF
GOLDEN
ROD

PRAIDIE
BLAZING
STAR

YELLOW
CONE
FLOWER

YELLOW
CONE
FLOWER

WILD
BERGAMOT

ROSIN
WEED

LAND

PURPLE CONE FLOWER

STIFF
COREOPSIS

WILD
QUININE

WILD
QUININE

WHITE
WILD
INDIGO

LE
FLOWER

FOXGLOVE
BEARD
TONGUE

RATTLE
SNAKE
MASTED

PALE
PURPLE

PRAIDIE SMOKE

AROMATIC
ASTER

FLOWER

WEED

SHOOTING STAR

WILD
BERGAMOT

UM ROOT

PRAIDIE
DOCK

LITTLE
BLUE
STEM

WILD
QUININE

PRAIDIE
BLAZING
STAR

YELLOW
CONE
FLOWER

PURPLE
CONE
FLOWER

RATTLE
SNAKE
MASTED

STIFF
COREOPSIS

PRAIDIE
SNOKE
AND
SHOOTING
STAR

FOX
GLOVE
BEARD
TONGUE

STIFF
GOLDEN
ROD

COMPASS
PLANT

WILD
QUININE

PALE
PURPLE
CONE
FLOWER

SMOOTH
BLUE
ASTER

INDIAN
GRASS

PRAIDIE
ALUM
ROOT

BUTTERFLY
WEED

STIFF
GOLDEN
ROD

PRAIDIE
DROP
SEED

**Purple Coneflower and
Yellow Coneflower
dominate the July border.**

DESIGN FOR NATIVE PLANTS AT A GAS STATION

HERE'S AN EXAMPLE of a native plant design I created for a gas station a few years ago. I planted 'Gro-low' Sumac under the required trees and filled in the sunny areas with Shrubby Potentilla, Purple Coneflower, Prairie Blazing Star, Showy Black-eyed Susan, Prairie Dropseed, and Switch Grass. ❧

Prairie Blazing Star and Showy Black-eyed Susan bloom in front of 'Northwind' Switch Grass at this gas station.

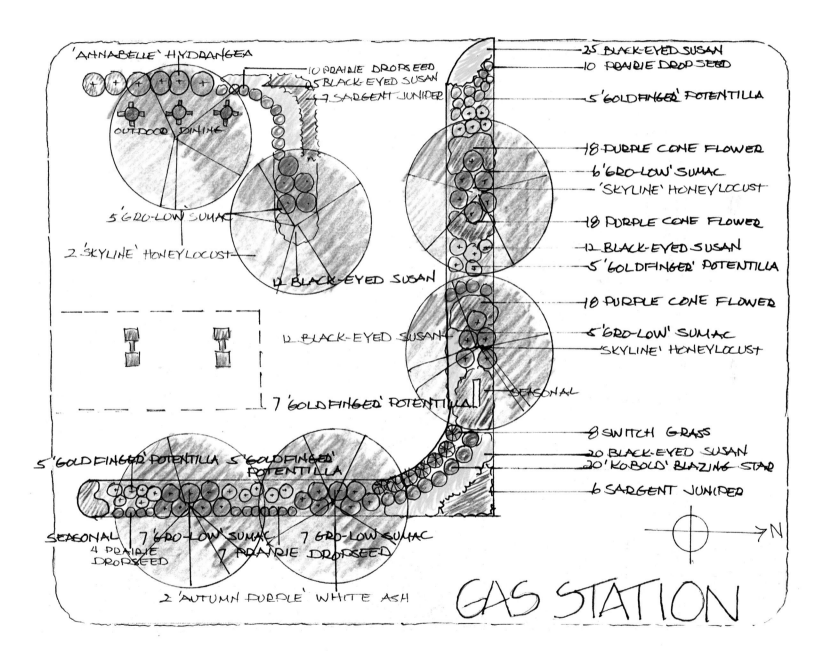

'ANNABELLE' HYDRANGEA

10 PRAIRIE DROPSEED
25 BLACK-EYED SUSAN
7 SARGENT JUNIPER

OUTDOOR DINING

5 'GRO-LOW' SUMAC

2 'SKYLINE' HONEYLOCUST

12 BLACK-EYED SUSAN

12 BLACK-EYED SUSAN

7 'GOLDFINGER' POTENTILLA

SEASONAL

5 'GOLDFINGER' POTENTILLA   5 'GOLDFINGER' POTENTILLA

SEASONAL   7 'GRO-LOW' SUMAC   7 'GRO-LOW' SUMAC
4 PRAIRIE   7 PRAIRIE DROPSEED
DROPSEED

2 'AUTUMN PURPLE' WHITE ASH

25 BLACK-EYED SUSAN
10 PRAIRIE DROP SEED

5 'GOLDFINGER' POTENTILLA

18 PURPLE CONE FLOWER
6 'GRO-LOW' SUMAC
'SKYLINE' HONEYLOCUST

18 PURPLE CONE FLOWER
12 BLACK-EYED SUSAN
5 'GOLDFINGER' POTENTILLA

18 PURPLE CONE FLOWER
5 'GRO-LOW' SUMAC
'SKYLINE' HONEYLOCUST

8 SWITCH GRASS
20 BLACK-EYED SUSAN
20 'KOBOLD' BLAZING STAR
6 SARGENT JUNIPER

N

GAS STATION

DESIGN FOR A DRY HILL PRAIRIE GARDEN

YOU CAN CREATE a colorful and interesting entryway to a home formed by a semicircular driveway. Mound up the soil in the area for dramatic effect, then clothe it with prairie plants that are indigenous to hill prairies. Use a light soil, mixed with some sand or even gravel. The drainage must be perfect. Add limestone ledges or outcropping to create even more interest, if you wish. Because this garden is seen most often from a car, use showy plants in large drifts that will show off from a distance.

This garden has year-round interest, beginning in spring with coral-pink Prairie Smoke, golden Heart-leaved Meadow Parsnip, and Prairie Alum Root, followed by drifts of mauve

Pale Purple Coneflower, which blooms in June and July. Stiff Coreopsis adds its luminous gold in late June, continuing into July along with Prairie Cinquefoil. Purple Prairie Clover blooms in July; the lacy Prairie Baby's Breath and lavender-blue Wild Petunia begin to bloom in July, continuing through August. Drifts of purple Aromatic Aster fluff and billow along the verge in September and into October, a dramatic contrast with copper-colored Little Blue Stem. Clumps of bronze and copper Prairie Dropseed also add to the fall and winter picture.

Hillsides drain faster than flat land and require places that can survive with little moisture. ❧

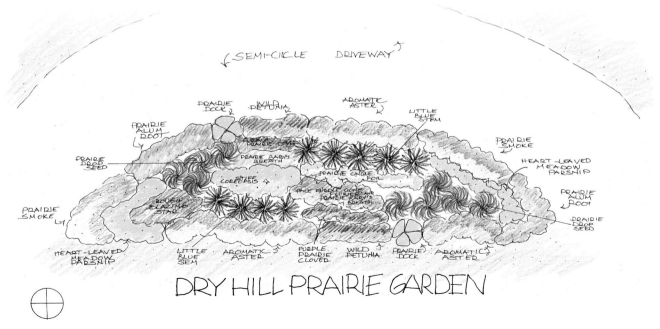

DRY HILL PRAIRIE GARDEN

Above left: Stiff Coreopsis and Prairie Baby's Breath bloom in July next to outcropping.

Above right: The copper stems and feathery seeds of Little Blue Stem are a perfect foil for the purple Aromatic Aster in September and October.

Below left: Showy Aromatic Aster provides the final show in October in this berm garden. The foliage of Stiff Coreopsis has turned scarlet, while the dark brown cones of Purple Coneflower dot the landscape.

Below right: Purple Coneflower, Prairie Baby's Breath, and Stiff Coreopsis provide color to the shallow hill in July. The grass in the rear is exotic Maiden Grass from a previous planting.

DESIGN FOR AN EAST-FACING SLOPE UNDER TREES WITH OUTCROPPING

THIS EAST-FACING HILLSIDE, shaded by large White Oaks, was filled with weeds and even some Crown Vetch the first time I saw it. After removing the weedy groundcover, limestone outcropping was installed and then planted with native plants that thrive on rocky slopes. I began with three Common Witch Hazel (*Hamamelis virginiana*), an open, multi-stem shrub or small tree, 10′ to 12′ tall, with horizontal branches, indigenous to wooded slopes throughout the eastern half of our country. The bright green, toothed leaves turn to glorious gold in October, but it gets even better. A tangle of narrow golden ribbons unfold in October, but they are not noticeable until the matching golden leaves fall at the end of October. Then the fragrant, spidery, yellow flowers show off magnificently against the bare brown branches, maintaining bloom into December.

The Dwarf Bush-honeysuckle (*Diervilla lonicera*) is often found with Paper Birch and Witch Hazel. It is not a true honeysuckle, however—its June and July yellow tubular blossoms only resemble those of honeysuckle. Its most spectacular feature is its autumn purple and yellow foliage. It is a low-growing, rambling shrub, 1′ to 3′ tall, found most often on rocky east- and north-facing slopes. If Dwarf Bush-honeysuckle is unavailable, consider using Splendens Bush Honeysuckle (*Diervilla x splendens*), a hybrid between *Diervilla lonicera* and *Diervilla sessilifolia*, the Southern Bush Honeysuckle, which

seems to be readily obtainable commercially

I then followed with drifts of 'Gro-low' Sumac and Illinois Rose, accented with three spectacular Spikenard. I filled in among the rocks with clumps of Wild Columbine and The Wild Columbine and Tufted Hair Grass bloom in May and June, followed by Foxglove Beard Tongue and Splendens Bush Honeysuckle in June; the Illinois Rose and Spikenard bloom in July. In August the rose produces copious quantities of red berries, which hang on most of the winter, while the Spikenard forms huge clusters of burgundy berries.

But the most spectacular show begins in autumn with the fiery foliage of the trees and shrubs is complemented by the lavender-blue asters and radiant yellow goldenrod. The Bush Honeysuckle becomes burgundy and amber; the Witch Hazel turns to gold, while Gro-low Sumac bursts into flame. Incredibly, the foliage of the Illinois Rose becomes glossy scarlet, the most beautiful of all. ❧

There is a remarkable nobility in rocks, weather-beaten and worn by water of past ages. Rocks, like trees, have character all their own, and this character is emphasized when the rock is rightly placed.

—Jens Jensen, *Siftings*

Above left: Workman clear hillside of weeds.

Above right: Installation of rock outcropping.

Below left: Tufted Hair Grass blooms in June.

Below right: The fiery leaves of 'Gro-low' Sumac cover the ground beneath Common Witch Hazel.

Illinois Rose is found along woodland edges and in limestone areas.

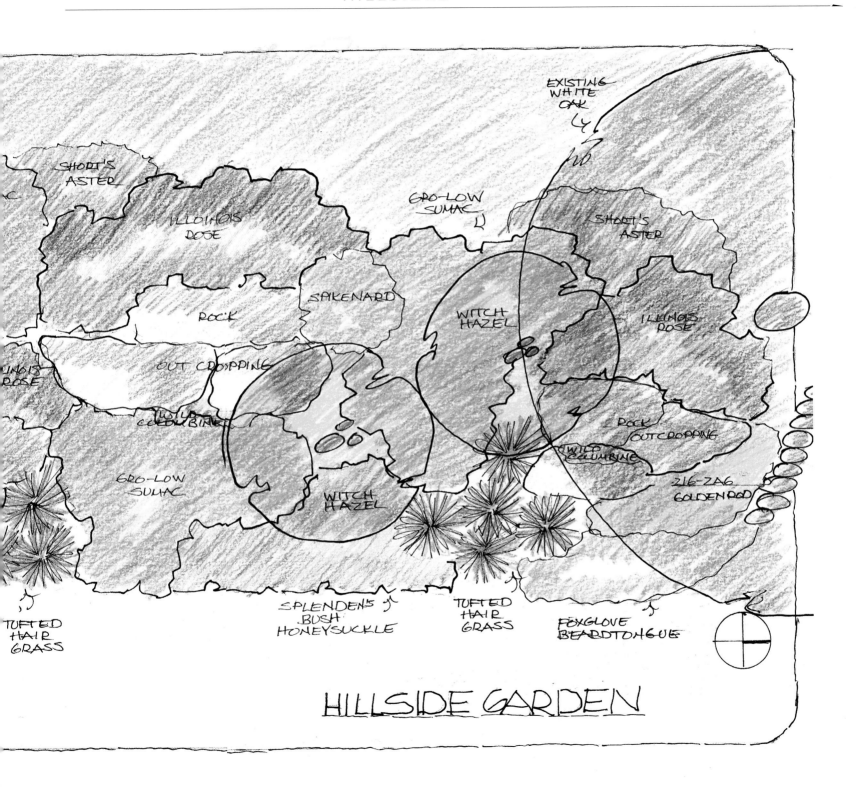

HILLSIDE GARDEN

DESIGN FOR A SHADED ROCKY SLOPE

WHILE IT IS DIFFICULT to buy a Paper Birch today, if one exists on your property, consider planting Witch Hazel and Dwarf Honeysuckle nearby. Then underplant the trees with the shrubby vines of Red Honeysuckle and Yellow Honeysuckle. For spring flowers and interesting foliage, add Sharp-lobed Hepatica, Wood Betony, Early Meadow Rue, Wild Columbine, Wild Stonecrop, Bulblet Fern, and Yellow Pimpernel. Yellow Pimpernel (*Taenidia integerrima*) resembles Heart-leaved Meadow Parsnip and Golden Alexanders, but the flower umbels are larger and more open, mustard yellow rather than canary yellow. It blooms in open woodlands from late May until the end of June.

Here's another design for a shaded rocky slope that uses much of the same plant material.

Left: The foliage of Common Witch Hazel turns to glowing gold in autumn.

Right: The leaves of the magnificent Paper Birch also become radiant gold in fall.

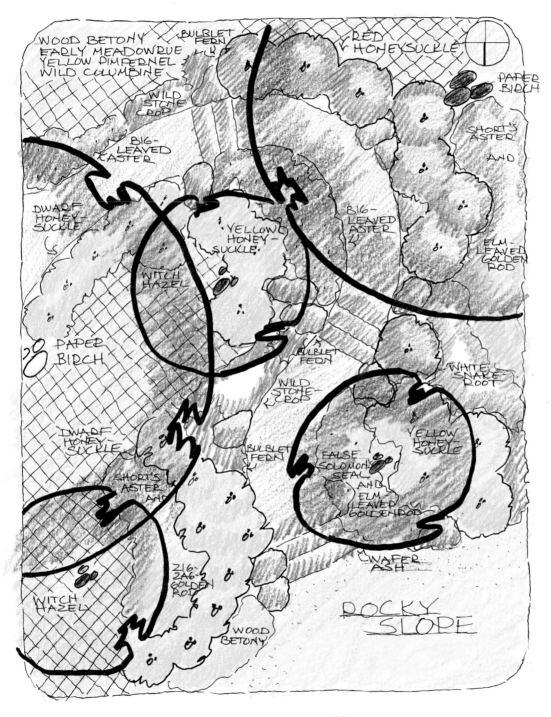

DESIGN FOR A SUNNY SOUTH-FACING TERRACED SLOPE

THIS IS A DESIGN based on one I created many years ago for a south-facing slope that had formerly been planted with pinks, iris, and coral-bells, but had become overrun with weeds. I had the slope terraced with low retaining walls made of limestone and then planted the terraces with many of the same plants that I used in and about my stone terrace, with stunning results.

At least two forbs are in bloom at any one time throughout the growing season. Prairie Smoke and Shooting Star begin to bloom in April and May, followed by Prairie Alum Root in May and June. The languid cups of Missouri Evening Primrose bloom in June, while Wild Petunia, Purple Prairie Clover, Nodding Wild Onion, and Cylindrical Blazing Star flower in July and August. Old-field Goldenrod and Purple Love Grass bloom in August and September. The garden is punctuated by clumps of Bicknell's Sedge, Side-oats Grama, Prairie Dropseed, and Little Bluestem.

These showy plants all have an affinity for limestone. They billow and foam over the stones in puffs and plumes of pink, mauve, and lavender, with a few chartreuse and golden accents, to make a cool, Monet-like composition. ❧

Left : Purple Coneflower and Butterfly Weed bloom adjacent to the house, while Wild Petunia flowers next to the stairs.

Right: Wild Petunia and Purple Prairie Clover bloom in sunny terrace in July.

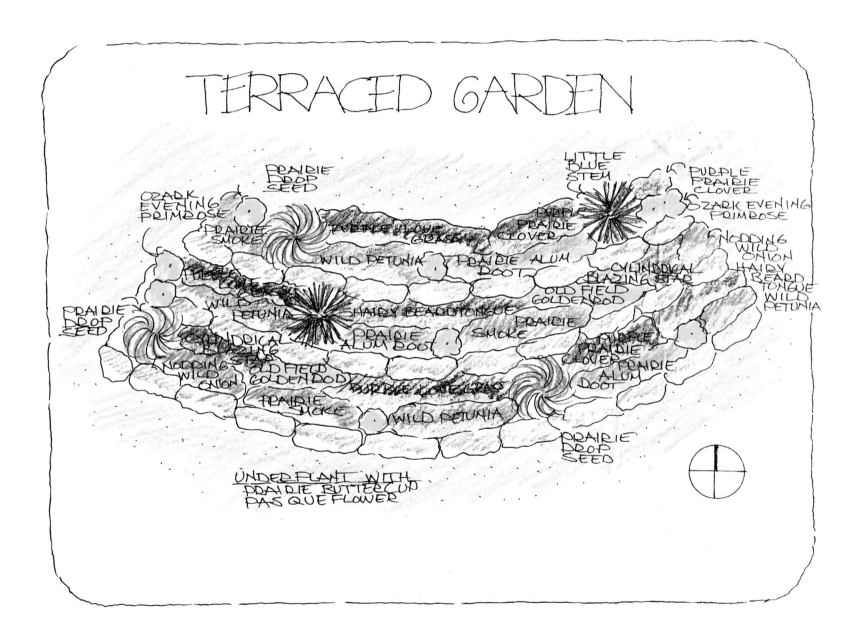

page 113

Chapter Six

WOODLANDS

The old oaks in the woodlot are without issue.

—Aldo Leopold, *A Sand County Almanac*

OAKS, REGRETTABLY, ARE not reproducing themselves in the wild. Prior to European settlement, the grasses in the savannas burned just as they did in the prairies, keeping woody plants from taking hold. But the suppression of fire plus the introduction of aggressive, exotic shrubs has spelled ruin for our oak savannas. They are now choked with the European Buckthorn (*Rhamnus cathartica*), a shrub or small tree, and the Amur and Tartarian Honeysuckle (*Lonicera maackii* and *tatarica*) shrubs. Birds distribute the seed of the buckthorn; it will become the exclusive understory shrub in disturbed or grazed woodland. The honeysuckles flower prettily in May, but their aggressive weediness soon chokes out native plants. "It would be difficult to exaggerate the weedy potential of this shrub," say Floyd Swink and Gerould Wilhelm of the Amur Honeysuckle in *Plants of the Chicago Region*. Both the buckthorn and the honeysuckle leaf out early and abscise their leaves late, thereby allowing very little sunlight to reach ground level. All this shade has kept oak trees from reproducing, guaranteeing their eventual demise. The dense cover also keeps native wildflowers from sprouting and growing on the woodland floor. Without an herbaceous carpet, the soil will soon erode away. In addition, trees rely on the deep fibrous roots of herbaceous plants to keep them adequately hydrated.

. . . on the fertile Corn Belt soils, all our oaks are headed for oblivion, except where ecological restoration or other intentional management protects them.

—Stephen Packard, "Interseeding,"
The Tallgrass Restoration Handbook

Tall herbaceous plants, such as Purple Joe Pye Weed, can provide privacy in both summer and winter.

A key first step to restore a savanna is to remove all brush that is choking the oaks. The buckthorn and honeysuckle have to be cut to the ground, and the stumps must be herbicided; otherwise the shrubs grow back with renewed vigor.

The next step is a controlled burn to get rid of the exotic groundcover such as Garlic Mustard, seedlings of maple, ash, and box elder trees, and the accumulation of leaf and stick litter. Once light and rain reaches the woodland floor, the dormant seed bank that's already in the soil may sprout and grow. If, however, there's been much erosion, the seed bank may be gone and the savanna will have to be re-seeded.

Many people don't want to remove the buckthorn and honeysuckle from their savannas and woodlands because of the privacy the shrubs afford from roads and neighbors. But tall herbaceous plants such as Purple Joe Pye Weed, Pale-leaved Sunflower, False Sunflower, Sweet Black-eyed Susan, Tall Coreopsis, Great St. John's Wort, and Purple Giant Hyssop, all of which grow 5′ to 8′ tall, can be planted around the periphery of a property to provide some screening the first year. Then plant trees and shrubs along the edge that will offer complete privacy within a few years.

Shingle Oak, with its persistent leaves, will work well in dry savannas and woodlands. Ironwood, with smaller leaves that also persist through the winter, will afford a certain amount of privacy, as well. Both of these trees can be purchased in either tree or shrub form. The dense branching pattern of American Hazelnut, Gray Dogwood, or any of the arrowwoods make additional good choices for screening the edges of Bur and White Oak woodlands.

While woodlands in the countryside are overgrown with weedy, woody shrubs, the opposite is true of the upscale,

Three Methods for Removing Buckthorn and Honeysuckle from Savannas and Woodlands

➤ **Cut Buckthorn to the ground and immediately paint cut surfaces with the herbicide Garlon-3A during the growing season or Garlon-4 during the winter. Garlon is not available at garden centers; you must obtain it from forestry or farm supply stores. Brush-B-Gone is a lower concentration of herbicide that may work as well. Roundup isn't effective on Buckthorn.**

➤ **Cut Honeysuckle to the ground in the fall; the following spring, paint or spray the new growth that emerges with Roundup.**

➤ **Cover the stumps of the cut-down trees/shrubs with heavy black plastic; they will eventually die.**

➤ **You can also girdle the tree; it will die in two years, top and roots.**

"wooded" sections of our towns and suburbs, which are also oak savannas. Not only are the shrubs cleared out but also the herbaceous groundcover; and a Kentucky Blue Grass lawn has been installed beneath the trees. While there is enough light under the canopy of an oak tree to maintain a lawn, it is more ecologically sound and infinitely prettier to instead grow wildflowers and grasses under its spreading branches. Trees are healthier when deep-rooted herbaceous plants draw water down into the soil. Trees grow $1^{1}/2$ times faster when grown in beds than when planted singly in the lawn, according to Connor Shaw, owner of Possibility Place Nursery in Monee, Illinois. ❧

A WOODLAND SCOURGE: GARLIC MUSTARD

I WAS DISHEARTENED by the seemingly endless, exclusive colonies of Garlic Mustard (*Alliaria petiolata*) that inhabited the verges of Sleepy Hollow Road, a shady, four-mile country road between Elgin and Dundee. But amazingly, I suddenly saw a long stretch of the lovely, native Toothwort in full bloom at the edge of the road that hadn't (yet) been overrun by the aggressive Garlic Mustard. The takeover by Garlic Mustard is a rather recent phenomenon. The colonies have overrun extensive areas of disturbed, shady places, especially floodplains of streams, wooded floodplains, and roadsides. Garlic Mustard is an aggressive seeder. Its large leaves shade the ground and prevent other wildflowers from sprouting, so it soon becomes an exclusive stand.

Since Garlic Mustard is a biennial, its flower tops have to be whacked off before it sets seed, in order to stop its cycle of flower, seed, and new seedlings that winter over to flower the next year. However, it quickly flowers and sets seed again after its first decapitation; so the process must be repeated. The beheaded flowers will also set seed. The best solution is an autumnal woodland burn, says Gerould Wilhelm. ❧

LEAVES

O wild West Wind, thou breath of Autumn's being,
Though, from whose unseen presence the leaves dead
Are driven, like ghosts from an enchanter fleeing.
—Percy Bysshe Shelley, *"Ode to the West Wind"*

FALLEN LEAVES ARE NOWADAYS referred to as "landscape waste." That must be quite a shock to Mother Nature, who thought dead leaves were mulch and fertilizer for the trees from which they fell. What was once beneficial and sustainable is now a "problem" that seemingly can only be solved by government. (People who want less government in their lives apparently suspend their philosophy during the month of October when they demand that their municipality remove the leaves from their private property and haul them out of sight.)

So now we have the leaf (oops—landscape waste) removal trucks touring the entire city, stopping at every house; this is in addition to the garbage truck and the recycling truck and the occasional large appliance-removal truck. We do this because the smoke from burning leaves pollutes the air, while everyone knows the exhaust from starting and stopping trucks does not.

Mother Nature does have a way of dealing with "landscape waste"—it is called decomposition. In our culture of instant gratification, though, decomposition takes way too much time. Perhaps some scientist will invent trees whose leaves decay before they hit the ground and spare us all of the inconvenience.

Or is it just possible that the problem lies in the way we landscape, growing trees within vast, manicured lawns where fallen leaves are considered unsightly?

Ideally, a tree ought to grow in a bed at least the size of its canopy, where its leaves can fall and remain. As the fallen leaves decompose, they become incorporated into the soil as organic matter. The soil will become more humusy and, as a bonus, it will become a perfect medium for growing savanna and woodland wildflowers and grasses. As I mentioned before, and it bears repeating, trees are healthier when the ground under them is carpeted with deep-rooted herbaceous plants. The plants will pull water down into the soil where the deep roots of the tree are able to draw upon it; in addition, the constant decay of the wildflower roots provides food for the trees.

People spend hundreds of dollars on wood mulch every few years to be spread under their shrubs to keep down weeds and to keep the soil from drying out; then they go to great effort and/or expense to blow away every last leaf that falls under those shrubs in autumn. Leaves are nature's mulch—they do the same thing as the wood mulch one buys, and they are free. In addition, the leaves break down and fertilize the shrubs; so you don't have to buy expensive mulch or fertilizer.

I live on a small property, only 50' by 125', and the leaves from several mature maples and ashes in the neighborhood fall or blow onto my lot. My grandchildren, who live in new subdivisions without fully developed trees, beg to come over to rake leaves and to jump in them. They bury themselves in the leaves, throw them about, and just generally have fun with them. I then use the leaves to create new planting beds for my ever-increasing prairie and savanna (see below). If you have no immediate use for the leaves, compost them in a simple wire container. ❧

Fallen leaves are referred to as landscape waste that needs to be gotten rid of as soon as possible.

Look upon leaves as mulch and fertilizer, not as a waste product that has to be hauled away. Your trees and shrubs will be healthier; you will have less lawn to mow, fewer leaves to rake, and areas in which to grow native wildflowers. ❧

Decomposition is the basic process that revitalizes the Earth.
—Janet Morinelli, *Stalking the Wild Amaranth*

NEW PLANTING BEDS

IF YOU WANT TO CREATE new planting beds for shrubs and/or flowers and grasses where the lawn is now, the ideal time is in autumn when the leaves fall. Outline the selected area with a garden hose, making broad curves; then cover the area inside with several thicknesses of newspaper pages and hold them down with stones, bricks, or heavy sticks. Then cover the area with thin leaves, such as those of maple or ash. You might want to surround the area with a low wire fence to keep the leaves (and newspaper) from blowing away-your neighbors will be grateful. That's it! By spring, the grass under-

neath will have died, and the leaves will be decomposing. Cut holes through the newspaper (it will eventually decay, also, since it is made of trees) in order to dig holes in the soil for your new plants. It really works! I created all my savanna gardens and one of my prairie gardens using this method. ❧

The ground was blanketed with wet leaves of every hue from livid crimson to flame-yellow, all their colors intensified by the wet and frost and wan morning sunlight.

—James Alexander Thom, *Follow the River*

Right: Before. I wanted to create new gardens in this grassy area.

Above left: The new planting area is marked off with a hose and newspapers spread over the grass in order to kill it.

Above right: Leaves are piled over the newspapers.

Below left: The following spring plants are planted into the area where the sod has been killed.

Below right: Savanna island with spring wildflowers in bloom, notably Wild Blue Phlox.

DESIGN FOR A SAVANNA BORDER WITH ISLAND

INSTEAD OF TRYING TO GROW Kentucky Blue Grass under the trees in your yard, why not plant a savanna instead? I did exactly that using the newspaper and leaves procedure outlined above. Located on the far side of the garage, the space is 32′ wide and 50′ deep. Shaded in the rear by the neighbor's American Elm, the area is shady at the back corner, partially shady in the middle, and sunnier toward the front next to the sidewalk.

We must have giants leaping out at us from the shadows to keep our senses alert after all those smooth undulating border schemes, and one such plant which begins its display towards the end of August is Eupatorium purpureum.
—Stephen Lacey, *The Startling Jungle*

The entrances to the garden are through an arched trellis from the sidewalk or on a path from the driveway. A Black Haw was installed next to the arch; a Prairie Rose climbs up one side of the trellis; a Gold Flame Honeysuckle clambers up the other side.

Three Pagoda Dogwood were positioned around the perimeter of the space. An 'Annabelle' Hydrangea was placed next to the near corner of the garage. The pleated, five-fingered leaves of Common Cinquefoil weave through the glossy leaves of Foxglove Beard Tongue and Cynthia for a stunning groundcover under the Hydrangea, blending into Penn Sedge, Wild Ginger, and various ferns and spring wildflowers that grow along the north side of the garage, terminating at another

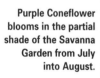

Purple Coneflower blooms in the partial shade of the Savanna Garden from July into August.

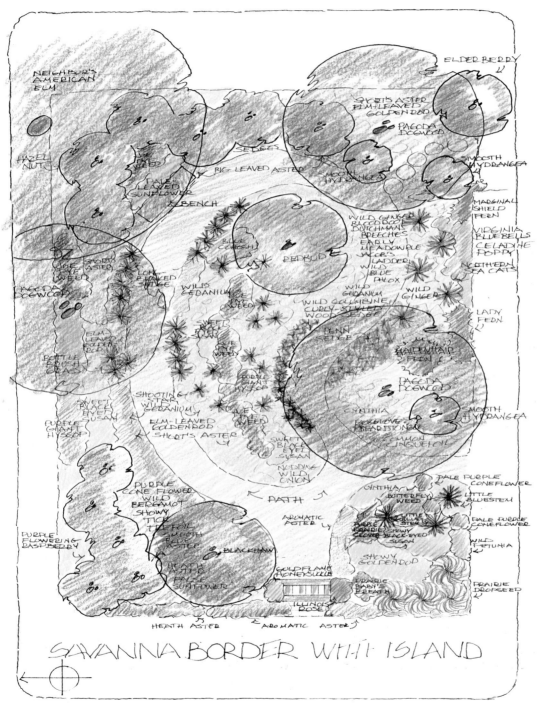

SAVANNA BORDER WITH ISLAND

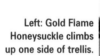

Left: Gold Flame Honeysuckle climbs up one side of trellis.

Right: Illinois Rose climbs up other side of trellis.

'Annabelle' Hydrangea. A third Hydrangea grows nearby along with an Elderberry (*Sambucus canadensis*). Huge, lacy, flat-topped, creamy-white flower clusters cover the Elderberry from mid-June through July. The flowers are followed by green berries that turn to cranberry, then luscious purple in August and September. The ripe berries make delicious preserves, jelly, pies, or wine. Large, bright-green compound leaves provide a lush, verdant background for the blossoms. Elderberry is a multistemmed, colonizing shrub, with un-branched arching stems that grow 8′ to 12′ tall.

American Hazelnut (*Corylus americana*) sashays along the back lot line and around the farthest corner under the elm. From early March until mid-April, golden pollen spills from the pendulous male catkins lighting up savannas, woodland edges, and fencerows. Growing 8′ to 10′ tall, Hazelnut forms colonies by means of root sprouts. In September and October it produces downy clusters of edible nuts, similar, or some say superior, to the commercial variety. The nuts are extremely attractive to birds and other wildlife, however; it's difficult to harvest the nuts before the critters do. In autumn the leaves turn to vermilion, apricot, and gold. Before European settlement it was the most prominent shrub in the Chicago region. But the suppression of fire and the overgrowth of exotic honeysuckle and buckthorn has altered the composition of open savannas to the extent that Hazelnut is rarely found in the wild any more. Fortunately, it is readily available from nurseries and it makes a splendid shrub for home grounds.

I placed a wire bench in the far back corner backed up by colorful stands of Pale-leaved Sunflower and Purple Joe Pye Weed and underplanted with Short-headed Bracted Sedge and Big-leaved Aster. Oak savannas are thick with the fluffy mauve

An arched trellis marks the entrance to the savanna garden. The Black Haw on the left blooms in May.

Above left: The lacy Lady Fern is a delight in spring gardens.

Above right: Celandine Poppy combines with Maidenhair Fern and Virginia Bluebells along the north side of the garage for a charming spring picture.

Below left: Three 'Annabelle' Hydrangea grow along the garage.

Below right: Maidenhair fern grows with Celandine Poppy and Wild Ginger along north garage wall.

clouds of tall Purple Joe Pye Weed (*Eupatorium purpureum*) from mid- to late July through August. This stately 3′ to 8′ plant flourishes in savannas or woodlands that are kept cleared of brush by cutting or burning. Surprisingly, some sunflowers grow in oak savannas where they receive sun for only part of the day. Pale-leaved Sunflower (*Helianthus strumosus*), so named because the undersurface of its leaves has a whitish bloom, is common in open woods and fencerow thickets. Radiant golden daisies bloom at the top of 3′- to 4′-tall stems beginning in late July and lasting through August and into September. An aggressive plant, it needs to be situated among other strong growers such as Purple Joe Pye Weed, White Snakeroot, Elm-leaved Goldenrod, and Short's Aster. Ornamental clumps of Long-beaked Sedge grow at the edge of the gardens. I encouraged Virginia Creeper to climb up the elm tree.

As the border led away from the shade, I added more drifts of Purple Joe Pye Weed and Pale-leaved Sunflower plus Purple Giant Hyssop, Sweet Black-eyed Susan, Short's Aster, White Snakeroot, and Great St. John's Wort. The blossoms of Purple Giant Hyssop (*Agastache scrophulariaefolia*) aren't purple, but very pale lavender; it is, however, a "giant"—the square stems grow up to 8′ tall, topped with dense spikes of tubular flowers from mid-July to mid-September. The numerous stamens that protrude from each individual blossom give the spike a fringed appearance. Umber-yellow, brown-centered, long-stalked daisies bloom in clusters at the top of 4′ to 5′ stems of Sweet Black-eyed Susan (*Rudbeckia subtomentosa*) from late July through mid-September. Its name refers not to fragrant flowers, but to the anise aroma of the mature seed heads. It colonizes slowly, forming large clumps. In the wild, it is found at the edge of moist woodlands or thickets next to

Above: The fall foliage of American Hazelnut turns to vermilion, apricot, and gold.

Below: Blue-stemmed Goldenrod and Bottlebrush Grass grow next to wire bench.

Above left: White Snakeroot, Elm-leaved Goldenrod , and Bottlebrush Grass bloom in the autumn savanna.

Above right: Purple Joe Pye Weed, Sweet Black-eyed Susan, Purple Giant Hyssop, and Purple Coneflower are stunning in the August savanna garden.

Below left: Purple Joe Pye Weed and Pale-leaved Sunflower bloom along a tall border in the late summer savanna.

Below right: WIld Bergamot and Showy Tick Trefoil bloom in sun or part shade in July.

prairies. It makes a complementary companion to Purple Joe Pye Weed.

Drifts of Shooting Star, Cynthia, Common Cinquefoil, and more sedge ran along the verge. Purple Flowering Raspberry filled in the corner near the sidewalk, along with matching Purple Coneflower. I added Showy Tick Trefoil and Wild Bergamot to the mix to enhance the rose-purple theme. Smooth Blue and Heath Aster soon infiltrated the area, as well; Aromatic Aster found a new home along the sidewalk verge.

The next year, I carved out an island in the center of the area and planted a Redbud as a focal point. I planted a matrix of woodland sedges throughout the garden: low-growing Penn Sedge, Curly-styled Wood Sedge, and Purple-sheathed Graceful Sedge along with the larger Long-beaked Sedge and Short-headed Bracted Sedge, then added pockets of woodland wildflowers.

What one might assume to be clumps of grass in the woods are not grasses at all, but sedges. There are more than 150 species of sedge in Kane County where I live—most of it

Sedges Have Edges

"Sedges have edges" is a popular aphorism, referring to the solid triangular stems of sedges as opposed to the hollow round stems of grasses. It is not always true, but it is often enough to use as a reliable indicator to distinguish between sedges and grasses.

Above: Purple Joe Pye Weed, Elm-leaved Goldenrod, and Bottlebrush Grass bloom along edge of savanna garden in late summer.

Below: A large clump of Bottlebrush Grass with a self-seeded Garden Phlox.

Above: The diminutive fuchsia flowers of Redbud make it a focal point of a garden wherever it is.

Below: The open stars of Bloodroot are among the first wildflowers to open in savanna and woodland.

grows in woodland or wetland. But why plant sedges? Woodland wildflowers thrive in a matrix of sedges, declares Gerould Wilhelm. The root systems of sedges are denser than those of forbs, thereby absorbing and holding more water that makes the soil spongier and less likely to dry out.

The season begins with Bloodroot and Dutchman's Breeches in bloom in late March through early April; Virginia Bluebells, Celandine Poppy, and Bellwort in April; Jacob's Ladder, Wild Blue Phlox, Wild Geranium, Wild Columbine, and Virginia Waterleaf, along with the Black Haw and Pagoda Dogwood, follow in May.

The gold-centered, white-petaled open stars of Bloodroot (*Sanguinaria canadensis*) appear briefly in the open spring sunshine of rich woodlands as early as late March, their stems wrapped in loosely furled, large-lobed, kidney-shaped leaves. As the flowers shatter, the leaves unfold, making a pretty groundcover. Dutchman's Breeches (*Dicentra cucullaria*) open in April, a few days after the Bloodroot. Aptly named, upside-down pantaloons hang from arched stems that rise above bluish-green, fringed leaves. These, too, are ephemerals; the leaves disappear once the flowers have set seed. Not as fragile as the Bloodroot, the blossoms of Dutchman's Breeches will sometimes last into the month of May.

Virginia Bluebells (*Mertensia virginica*) are the showiest of the spring wildflowers. Its pink buds turn into nodding clusters of sky-blue bells on 18″ to 24″ stems that bloom profusely until mid-May or even longer in a cool spring. In the wild it is found in mesic woodlands and wooded floodplains, although on home grounds it will grow in drier situations. A prolific seeder, it will even expand into shady or partially shady lawns.

The large-$1^{1}/2''$ diameter-bright golden cupped flowers of

Canary-yellow Bellwort and Celandine Poppy shine among unfolding ferns at the Natural Garden in St. Charles, Illinois.

Above left: The charming Dutchman's Breeches bloom in the midst of the distinctive Bloodroot foliage.

Above right: Virginia Bluebells and Celandine Poppy carpet the ground in the woodland garden at The Natural Garden in St. Charles, IL.

Below left: Wild Blue Phlox is the showiest of the spring woodland wildflowers, in bloom in May.

Below right: WIld Geranium sows its seeds with abandonment, but never crowds out other plants.

Celandine Poppy (*Stylophorum diphyllum*) make a particularly striking picture when combined with blue-flowered plants such as Virginia Bluebells, Jacob's Ladder, or Wild Blue Phlox. A bushy perennial 15″ tall and wide, it begins to bloom in mid-April, continuing through May, with sporadic bloom throughout the summer. The attractive, deeply lobed, scalloped leaves eventually fade away. It is found most often in moist woods or on north-facing slopes. In home grounds it even grows in dry shade. Don't confuse it with the European biennial Celandine (*Chelidonium majus*), which at first glance looks similar, but has much smaller flowers and alternate leaves rather than opposite. It becomes a weed in shaded ground and crowds out native plants—if it is growing on your property, get rid of it.

The conspicuous, fragrant, lemon-yellow bells dangling from the arching stems of Bellwort or Great Merrybells (*Uvularia grandiflora*) are delightful. The 10″- to 15″-tall stem appears to perforate the shiny, bright-green, clasping leaves and gives a twisted appearance to the whole plant. Bellwort is found mostly in sloping, calcareous woodlands, blooming in April and May.

Jacob's Ladder (*Polemonium reptans*) is the first woodland wildflower I grew, given to me by my mother-in-law from her garden. The leafy clumps are decorated with clusters of nodding, china-blue cups that seed themselves cheerfully throughout the garden. One almost imagines that the pinnately compound leaves resemble a ladder.

Clusters of fragrant, lavender-blue, five-petaled blossoms bloom at the top of the 8″ to 12″ wiry stems of Wild Blue Phlox (*Phlox divaricata*). Wild Geranium (*Geranium maculatum*) begins to bloom in early to mid-May as the Virginia

Above: Purple Joe Pye Weed, Starry Campion, and Bottlebrush Grass make a charming composition in the savanna island.

Below: Purple Joe Pye Weed and Elm-leaved Goldenrod surround a wren house in the savanna island.

OAK LEAVES

OAK LEAVES PERSIST rather than decomposing as ash or maple leaves do—they are "born to burn" as Stephen Packard says in the Spring 2001 issue of Chicago Wilderness. Oak savannas and woodlands are fire-dependent; a controlled burn is needed to rid the area of weeds just as it is in prairies. Burn the leaves beneath the trees where they land—don't pile them up. The fire will kill the Blue Grass and other exotic plants, while releasing the native seed bank that might still be there. Following the burn, seed with appropriate grasses, sedges, and wildflowers just before the first snow or in spring. ❧

DESIGN FOR A BACKYARD SAVANNA

THIS SHALLOW BACK YARD, overhung by an umbrella of Bur Oak and Shagbark Hickory, was too shady to grow a lawn, so I suggested a carpet of sedges and low-growing wildflowers. A brick path meanders from the south side of the house to the brick terrace lined with Wild Ginger and clumps of Long-beaked Sedge. Ferns and sedges grow under the Shagbark Hickory that grows next to the house, while Tufted Hair Grass lines the outside edge of the patio. A matrix of woodland sedges with pockets of spring woodland flowers fills in the area under the ancient Bur Oak.

The property is adjacent to a common area that was choked with buckthorn. The trees were cut down and the stumps treated with herbicide. A controlled burn destroyed the exotic weeds and rid the area of sticks and leaves, allowing light and rain to penetrate the ground. The dormant seed bank in the soil was awakened by the fire and native plants began to sprout. Hundreds of Trout Lilies appeared the first spring followed by Pale Touch-me-nots in summer.

The conspicuously mottled, narrow leaves of the White Trout Lily or Dogtooth Violet (*Erythronium albidum*), which some might say resemble a speckled trout, appear on wooded slopes and bottomlands among oak leaves, forming large colonies. Most of the leaves grow singly, but the diminutive, nodding, white lily-shaped blossoms only spring up from paired leaves. It is fleeting-the leaves disappear by the end of May. There is a yellow-flowered form, also, *Erythronium americanum*, more commonly found east of Lake Michigan.

Pale Touch-me-not or Yellow Jewelweed (*Impatiens pallida*) is a charming, self-seeding, native annual. It grows 2' to 4' tall with pale yellow blossoms that dangle from the ends of arching stems from early July to early October. It seeds itself prolifically, with abundant seedlings emerging every spring. There is also an orange-flowered form. Both of these impatiens are found in mesic woodlands as well as shaded floodplains, calcareous fens, and low areas near streams and ponds. If the tiny seedpods are touched, the seeds are forcibly ejected and the pod curls up into a spiral—fun for children (and grown-ups) to experience. Jewelweed is frequently found growing

Brick path meanders
through new
woodland garden.

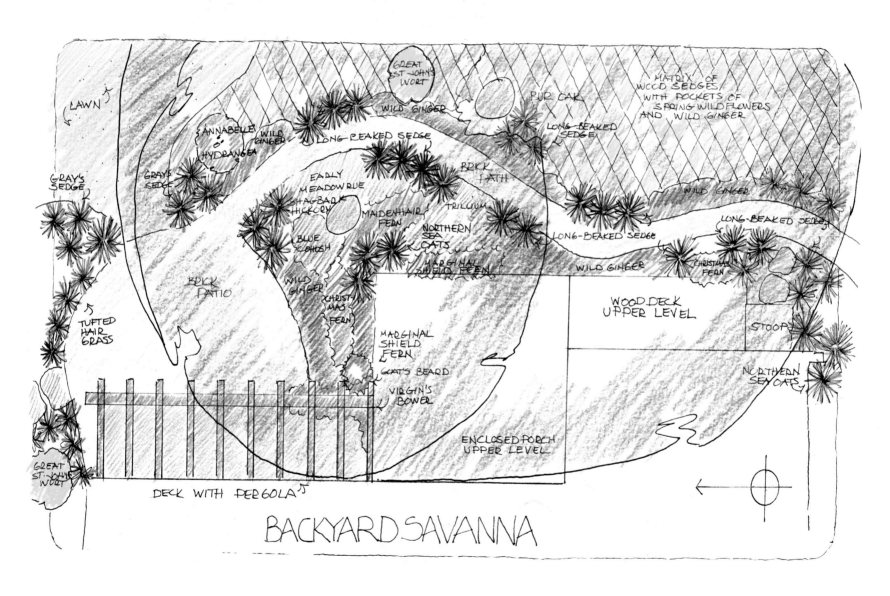

LAWN

GREAT ST JOHN'S WORT

WILD GINGER

MATRIX OF WOOD SEDGES WITH POCKETS OF SPRING WILDFLOWERS AND WILD GINGER

BUR OAK

ANNABELLE HYDRANGEA

WILD GINGER

LONG-BEAKED SEDGE

LONG-BEAKED SEDGE

GRAY'S SEDGE

GRAY'S SEDGE

BRICK PATH

WILD GINGER

EARLY MEADOWRUE

SHAGBARK HICKORY

MAIDENHAIR FERN

TRILLIUM

LONG-BEAKED SEDGE

BLUE COHOSH

NORTHERN SEA OATS

LONG-BEAKED SEDGE

MARGINAL SHIELD FERN

CHRISTMAS FERN

BRICK PATIO

WILD GINGER

WILD GINGER

CHRIST- MAS FERN

WOOD DECK UPPER LEVEL

STOOP

TUFTED HAIR GRASS

MARGINAL SHIELD FERN

GOAT'S BEARD

VIRGIN'S BOWER

NORTHERN SEA OATS

ENCLOSED PORCH UPPER LEVEL

GREAT ST JOHN'S WORT

DECK WITH PERGOLA

BACKYARD SAVANNA

with Poison Ivy. There is anecdotal evidence that Jewelweed is an antidote to the rash caused by Poison Ivy.

I then planted a mix of spring, summer, and fall forbs and grasses for three-season interest. ❧

Left: Hundreds of Trout Lily appeared after the controlled burn.

Right: Before garden was planted.

DESIGN FOR AN ISLAND SAVANNA GARDEN

HERE'S AN EXAMPLE of a savanna island I planted for some clients. I had the outlying savanna cleared of brush and then burned. The property owners were willing to wait for the native seed bank to grow back and flower. But this island was close to the house and driveway, so I wanted an immediate first-year show here. An immense Bur Oak, several smaller Red Oak, and some young Basswood remained after the buckthorn and honeysuckle were removed. I placed five Hazelnut randomly through the L-shaped area; then planted drifts of Joe Pye Weed, Pale-leaved Sunflower, and Purple Giant Hyssop through the center of the bed. In the sunnier west end of the garden, I planted prairie shrubs, forbs, and grasses and filled the shadier areas with plugs of savanna and woodland plants. This garden is continuously colorful, from the golden March catkins of the Hazelnut, through the spring-blooming woodland wildflowers and sedges, the summer spikes of the savanna grasses and forbs, and finally the fall asters and goldenrods and the red leaves of the oaks and hazelnuts. The trees, shrubs, and grasses have winter interest, as well. ❧

Left: Before—Oak savanna choked with buckthorn and honeysuckle.

Right: After—All the exotic shrubs have been cut down and herbicided.

Woodland island
new residence with
Purple Joe Pye Weed
and Elm-leaved
Goldenrod
in September.

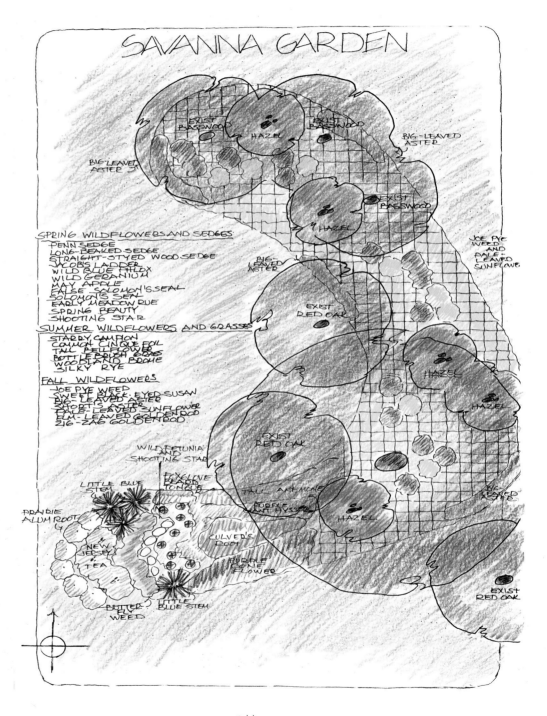

SAVANNA GARDEN

EXIST BASSWOOD

HAZEL

EXIST BASSWOOD

BIG-LEAVED ASTER

BIG-LEAVED ASTER

EXIST BASSWOOD

HAZEL

JOE PYE WEED AND PALE-LEAVED SUNFLOWER

BIG-LEAVED ASTER

EXIST RED OAK

HAZEL

HAZEL

SPRING WILDFLOWERS AND SEDGES
  PENN SEDGE
  LONG-BEAKED SEDGE
  STRAIGHT-STYED WOOD SEDGE
  JACOB'S LADDER
  WILD BLUE PHLOX
  WILD GERANIUM
  MAY APPLE
  FALSE SOLOMON'S SEAL
  SOLOMON'S SEAL
  EARLY MEADOW RUE
  SPRING BEAUTY
  SHOOTING STAR

SUMMER WILDFLOWERS AND GRASSES
  STARRY CAMPION
  COMMON CINQUEFOIL
  TALL BELLFLOWER
  BOTTLEBRUSH GRASS
  WOODLAND BROME
  SILKY RYE

FALL WILDFLOWERS
  JOE PYE WEED
  SWEET BLACK-EYED SUSAN
  BIG-LEAVED ASTER
  SHORT'S ASTER
  PALE-LEAVED SUNFLOWER
  ELM-LEAVED GOLDENROD
  ZIG-ZAG GOLDENROD

EXIST RED OAK

WILD PETUNIA AND SHOOTING STAR

FOXGLOVE BEARD TONGUE

TALL ANEMONE

BIG LEAVED

LITTLE BLUE STEM

PURPLE GIANT HYSSOP

HAZEL

PRAIRIE ALUM ROOT

CULVER'S ROOT

NEW JERSEY TEA

PURPLE CONE FLOWER

BUTTER FLY WEED

LITTLE BLUE STEM

EXIST RED OAK

Pale-leaved Sunflower and Purple Giant Hyssop grow in island next to house, in bloom in August.

NATIVE WILDFLOWER GARDEN

97-YEAR OLD VIRGINIA Umburger was ahead of her time— way ahead of her time. She eschewed a lawn among the scattered oaks that surrounded her newly built Cape Cod house (in 1947) on her $1/2$ acre property and planted instead native shrubs and myriads of wildflowers-not only in the backyard, but-gasp-in the front yard, as well! The property is located near Trout Park, a rare forested fen, now an Illinois Nature Preserve, from which many seeds were deposited by birds into her gardens.

Diminutive, luminous, bright-yellow flowers of the native Spicebush gleam above a vast carpet of False Rue Anemone. Spring Beauty, Toothwort, Sharp-lobed Hepatica, Bloodroot, Dutchman's Breeches, Twinflower, and Dogtooth Violet brighten the floor of her amazing gardens. Redbud and Bladdernut grow generously throughout her property. ❧

Left: Spring woodland wildflowers carpet the ground at Ginny's house.

Right: Earliest-blooming Sharp-lobed Hepatica bloom near a stone ledge.

A carpet of False Rue Anemone, surrounds the Spicebush that is covered with diminutive yellow flowers in early spring.

JENS JENSEN

THERE IS A STREET in a Saint Charles, Illinois, subdivision called Jens Jensen Lane, but I daresay hardly anyone on the street knows the identity of Jens Jensen; they probably assume he is a relative of the developer.

A strong, colorful character, Jens Jensen was the Midwest's foremost landscape architect, practicing from 1905 through 1951. He revolutionized landscape design in much the same way that Frank Lloyd Wright transformed architecture. Both practiced in the Chicago area, Wright mainly in Oak Park and River Forest, Jensen on the North Shore, principally in Highland Park and Glencoe, an area along Lake Michigan that is naturally wooded.

Jensen began his private practice at the turn of the century, a little later than Wright. He advocated the use of native plant materials grouped together in naturalistic designs, in direct opposition to the practice of the Victorian era, which featured exotic, showy plants, each placed individually in the lawn.

It was early morning when he called me to the open door where he was standing out over a clearing. There was a peculiar light over this little sun opening, caused by the reflection of the sunrise. The clearing was bordered by a simple composition of hardwoods with a few hawthorn, crab-apples, and gray dogwood scattered on the edge. The light had added an enchantment to this simple composition, and Lindsay, watching this, said to me, "Such poems as this I cannot write."

—Jens Jensen, *Siftings*

A native of Denmark, Jensen as a boy took part in the

Left: Stratified limestone rock on Fox River in Batavia, IL.

Right: Stratified rock wall built by Jensen.

Horizontal lines of
the hawthorn—Jensen's
signature plant.

More shrubs with horizontal branching patterns favored by Jensen.

Above left: Blackhaw.

Right: American Highbush Cranberry grows next to a pergola at the Chicago Botanic Garden.

Below left: Pagoda Dogwood.

annual outdoor festivals that celebrated the changing seasons, as well as the sunrise festivals, summer concerts, and campfires that dated back to his country's pagan past (as he writes in his memoir, *Siftings*). This appreciation of the changing seasons and accompanying rituals influenced his design work, and, indeed, the course of his entire life. He believed a person should experience a garden by being in it, not just viewing it.

Wilhelm Miller, a horticulture professor at the University of Illinois, described the prairie movement in landscape gardening in an extension publication, *The Prairie Spirit in Landscape Gardening* (1915). He defined the "Prairie Style" as "employing three accepted principles of design-conservation of native scenery, restoration of local vegetation, and repetition of the horizontal line of land or sky, which is the strongest feature of prairie scenery."

Stratified horizontal lines were repeated in different materials, from layers of the native limestone rock to the horizontal branching patterns of the native hawthorn and crabapple to native perennials with flat-topped flowers. The Prairie School architects used the same forms in their houses, characterized by shallow, pitched-hip roofs, low, wide overhangs, and horizontal clusters of windows and banding on the walls.

While Jensen planned and planted many great estates, including those of Sears and Roebuck founder Julius Rosenwald in Highland Park, Illinois; Henry Ford in Dearborn, Michigan; the Edsel Ford estate in Grosse Pointe Shores, Michigan; he designed many smaller residential properties, as well.

He planted woodland edge shrubs in masses under tall trees around the perimeter of the backyard. The borders consisted of Black Haw Viburnum, Sheepberry, American High-

Jensen planted flat-topped prairie flowers such as this Wild Quinine.

House designed by
Frank Lloyd Wright
with horizontal lines.

bush Cranberry, American Hazelnut, Witch Hazel, Wild Plum, Pagoda Dogwood, Early Wild Rose, Ninebark, Gray Dogwood, Elderberry, Wild Crabapple, and Sumac. But the plant he used more than any other, and which came to symbolize him, was the native hawthorn. Low-branched, wider than tall, spreading to 30′, the horizontal branching pattern symbolized the prairie to Jensen. He placed them at promontories along the border of an opening or clearing, as a transition from woodland to meadow, or individually within larger meadows or savannas. Hawthorns flower in late May or early June with white roselike blossoms, effective for a week to 10 days.

The council ring was a recurring architectural element in Jensen's designs. A circular stone bench with a fire pit in the center, it was made with flagstone piers topped with large slabs of flagstone. It could have a diameter anywhere from 10′ to 20′

Above right: Hawthorn shrubs with the horizontal branching patterns favored by Jensen.

Below left: Ninebark blossoms resemble those of 'Van Houtte' Spirea, but Ninebark has more than one season of interest.

Below right: Rosy pedicels (flower and berry stems) add interest to Gray Dogwood in fall and early winter.

Smooth Sumac in its autumn tint—another favorite of Jensen.

or even larger. He situated the council rings within a woodland clearing or on a woodland edge with a view out toward a meadow, or on a promontory overlooking Lake Michigan. He enclosed them with the Iowa Crab and/or Wild Plum, underplanting the crabapple with common Woodland Violets and the plum with Virginia Bluebells.

The council ring was meant to inspire conversation, storytelling, drama, and singing around the campfire. In Jensen's words from *Siftings*, "In this friendly circle, around the fire, man becomes himself. Here there is no social caste. All are on the same level, looking each other in the face. A ring speaks of friendship and strength and is one of the great symbols of mankind. The fire in the center portrays the beginning of civilization..."

Another design element used by Jensen was sunlight and moonlight. He oriented his gardens east and west, so the owner could view the sunrise and sunset; he carved lanes through the trees through which the long shafts of light shone. He planted Sugar Maple and Sumac at the east end of a property so the setting sun would shine on them and set them on fire against the darkening sky. He created "sun openings" in woods, clearing an irregular space and bordering it with hawthorn, Iowa Crab, and Gray Dogwood. The sunlight made intriguing shadows as it moved throughout the day over the clearing. ❧

These trees were in their autumn tint, and the afterglow was a fiery red. Its reflection in the tops of these trees produced a light that to me made the trees seem to be afire. Ever since that time I have always tried to place the sugar maple or the sumac in such a situation that the evening light would set their tops aflame.
—Jens Jensen, *Siftings*

The Chicago Botanic Garden's interpretation of a Jens Jensen council ring.

TWO DESIGNS FOR A JENS JENSEN-STYLE BACKYARD

LARGE SWEEPS OF WOODLAND edge native shrubs, punctuated by hawthorns at regular intervals, surround a central lawn or "sun opening," a typical Jens Jensen design. The house is oriented east and west, along the path of the sun; shrubs with brilliantly colored fall foliage are situated along the western border that will be backlit by the setting sun. A hidden path, lined with savanna wildflowers, leads to a council ring along one side of the property; a lane on the other side leads to a small pool.

This backyard will have significance from the earliest

JENS JENSEN STYLE GARDEN

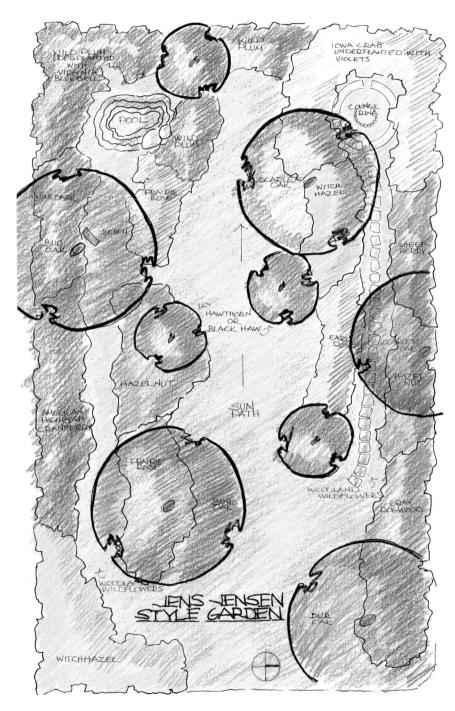

blooming American Hazelnut, followed by the spring and summer flowering shrubs, through the rich autumn coloring of the all the foliage. The interest continues with the fall and winter fruits and the notable horizontal branching pattern of the naked Hawthorns or Black Haws.

The second design, with similar shrubs and trees, has been adapted to the more typical suburban lot that has more width than depth. ❧

DESIGN FOR A FENCEROW

THIS SPLIT RAIL FENCE rambles along a heavily traveled road within the city limits. Joe Pye Weed and Woodland Sunflower mix at the back of the fence under the trees near the driveway entrance. American Hazelnut zigzags along the fence line; the bed then curves out in front of the fence into the sunlight where it's bright enough to grow prairie grasses-Switch Grass, Little Bluestem, and Prairie Dropseed. Aromatic Aster adds its purple daisies to the fall pallet. False Sunflower, Wild Bergamot, Smooth Blue Aster, New England Aster, and Foxglove Beard Tongue thrive in the partial shade next to the fence. Three Illinois Rose sprawl along the fence line, ravishing in July when it blooms and again in the fall and winter with its large hips and its stunning foliage ∾.

The little bluestem was exquisite with turquoise and garnet and chartreuse; and the big bluestem waved its turkeyfeet of deep purple high against the October sky, past the warm russet of the Indian grass.

In one long strip, a farmer was at work, taking down his fence.

"Why?" we asked.

"Easier to work it without fences," he answered. "If I ever want to turn stock into this field, it's easy to string up an electric fence."

That will be the end of that colorful rectangle of prairie, one foot wide, one-half mile long, and eight feet deep.

We picked a few purple turkeyfeet to take home. They make pleasant bookmarks in the old books.

—May Watts, *Reading the Landscape of America*

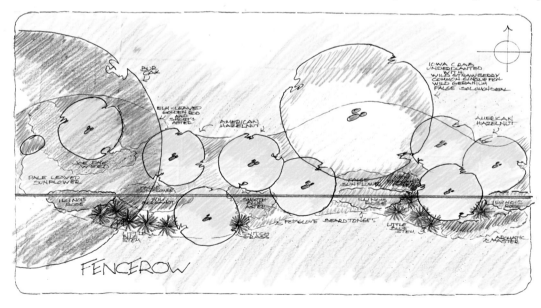

page 158

GREENWAYS

GET TOGETHER WITH your neighbors and jointly plant informal hedgerows along back and side property lines. Besides providing a continuous, bountiful harvest of flowers and berries, these plantings will attract birds and wildlife to the area. If enough people in a neighborhood do this, there will be a greenway through which animals may travel.

Tall trees typically found in fencerows are White Ash, Basswood, and White, Bur, or Red Oak; small trees could be Common Witch Hazel, Wild Crab, Downy and Cockspur Hawthorn, and Black Haw; common shrubs such as American Hazelnut, Gray Dogwood, Wild Plum, Early Wild Rose, Illinois Rose, Purple Flowering Raspberry, Elderberry, Nannyberry, Downy Arrowwood, and Choke Cherry; and vines such as Virginia Creeper, Yellow Honeysuckle, or Gold Flame Honeysuckle. Frequently found herbaceous plants are Wild Geranium, May Apple, Solomon's Seal, False Solomon's Seal, Drummond's Aster, Elm-leaved Goldenrod, and woodland grasses such as Bottlebrush Grass, Woodland Brome, and Silky Rye. ∾

Everything on this farm spells money in the bank.... There are no hedges, brush patches, fencerows, or other signs of shiftless husbandry. The cornfield has fat steers, but probably no quail. The fences stand on narrow ribbons of sod; whoever plowed that close to the barbed wires must have been saying, "Waste not, want not."

—Aldo Leopold, *A Sand County Almanac*

APRIL SHOWERS BRING MAY FLOWERS

FLOODING SEEMS TO GET worse every spring. Rainwater that has no place to infiltrate drains into rivers which then overflow their banks and devastate river towns, taking lives and destroying billions of dollars in homes and property. In 1996, the U.S. Army Corps of Engineers estimated that the damage caused by the flooding of the upper Des Plaines River averages more than $21 million dollars per year (Joel Greenberg, *A Natural History of the Chicago Region*).

This is not the way Mother Nature planned it.

She didn't know that so much of the earth would be built over and paved over, covered with roofs, roads, and parking lots that generate excessive loads of dirty water that have no place to go. She didn't know that farmers would install tile in their fields to drain the water and direct it into channeled drainage ditches, which empty into streams and rivers (90 percent of the wetlands in the Midwest have been drained by the laying of drain tile—"the single largest engineering feat in American history," says Ed Collins, a McHenry County ecologist).

The wet prairies were among the last to go, wrung out by long lines of clay tiles and bull ditches that hastened runoff and dropped the water table, drying the land for the plow.
  —John Madson,
    Where the Sky Began: Land of the Tallgrass Prairie

Prior to European settlement, deep-rooted prairie and savanna grasses and forbs absorbed all rainwater that did not evaporate. Only spring snowmelt that was unable to infiltrate into the still-frozen ground created excess water. But far from being a rushing torrent, it formed diffuse pools of water that flowed slowly across the landscape. The Des Plaines River today floods on a regular basis, but prior to European settlement, the northern section wasn't even channeled—it was part of a massive wetland. Where Salt Creek entered the area, it became the Kickapoo and headed southwest to join the Illinois River. In spring, the area between it and the Chicago River became inundated; and far from being considered a disaster, it was welcome because it allowed navigation between Lake Michigan and the Mississippi River (Floyd Swink and Gerould Wilhelm, *Plants of the Chicago Region*).

Whenever we disregard nature's rules, there is always a price to pay. But instead of altering our behavior to fit into the laws of nature, we turn to technology and engineering to find a way around the rules, which only works for a while.

Land use planners and engineers have, for the most part, designed swales, drainage ditches, culverts, and storm sewers to convey water as fast and as efficiently as possible away from where it falls. More and more impenetrable surfaces mean more and more dirty stormwater is directed into streams and rivers, carrying with it excessive fertilizers, herbicides, and pesticides from our overtreated lawns, oil and cadmium from our roads, and roof granules from our roofs.

Government bodies now require detention or retention ponds to be built in new developments to store stormwater, allow sediments to settle out, and then to release the water slowly into storm sewers, streams, and rivers in order to prevent flooding. But very little is being done to absorb rainwater where it falls as nature intended. We think of wetlands as depositories for excess stormwater but that's not the function of wetlands. Before human intrusion, wetlands were formed and maintained almost completely by groundwater discharge and direct precipitation (James M. Patchett and Gerould S. Wilhelm, *The Ecology and Culture of Water*).

There is a mechanism for federal protection of wetlands, but not of uplands, so government regulation concentrates only on preserving wetlands. "Article 1, section 8, of the U.S. Constitution ... gives Congress the power to regulate interstate commerce," which includes "migratory birds, navigable waterways, and wetlands adjacent to waterways," states Joel Greenberg in *A Natural History of the Chicago Region*. The federal Clean Water Act now discourages the filling in of wetlands, but almost all of the wetlands in Illinois have already been drained. A "wetland" is defined by the U.S. Army Corps of Engineers as an area that is "inundated or saturated by surface or ground water at a frequency and duration sufficient to support, and under normal circumstances [does] support, a prevalence of vegetation typically adapted for life in saturated soil conditions." "Normal circumstances" means no drain tile, so areas that were wetlands are still wetlands, even if they are temporarily drained dry. The Minnesota, Wisconsin, and Chicago areas are young landscapes—the last glacier retreated only 8,000 to 10,000 years ago. Because this region is poorly drained, it has one of the most diverse collections of wetlands in North America (Jerry Sullivan, *An Atlas of Biodiversity*).

In much of the Midwest, wetlands, and their beneficial contributions to water quality and erosion prevention, have been replaced by one of the most toxic surfaces humans have invented: the modern turf lawn. Gerould Wilhelm, noted

botanist and ecologist and former research taxonomist with the Morton Arboretum for 22 years, argues that turf grass is almost as impenetrable to rain as asphalt. Heavy rain, in particular, as we're wont to get in the Midwest, slips across the top of a thick Blue Grass turf and into storm sewers, ending up in the Gulf of Mexico, if not in someone's basement first. Prairie forbs and grasses will penetrate as much as 15 feet into the soil, enabling rainwater to be absorbed. A five-year-old planting of Switch Grass will absorb 8″ of rainfall per hour, according to landscape architect and hydrology engineer Jim Patchett. In contrast, the roots of Kentucky Blue Grass only penetrate into the ground a few inches, thereby increasing flooding, drainage, and the need for retention areas.

When stormwater is conveyed away from where it lands, very little water infiltrates our soil and recharges the groundwater. Unable to draw upon water reserves, the soil dries out

Left: This photo (courtesy of the Conservation Research Institute) compares the deep-rooted prairie plants with the shallowrooted Kentucky bluegrass as told in the text.

Page 160: Waterfall and creek at Coffee Creek in Chesterton, Indiana.

quickly, and then requires the installation of expensive irrigation systems. Incomprehensibly, we have designed drainage systems to carry away rainwater into streams and rivers and then installed irrigation systems to draw water back from the same river or lake to water our lawns and gardens. Doesn't it make more sense to keep our water (which is given to us for free) on our site in the first place? ❧

... an unusual and excessive amount of rain falling on a landscape sorely needing water, but stripped of its capacity to absorb it, both droughts and floods will continue to become more frequent and catastrophic.

—James M. Patchett and Gerould S. Wilhelm,
The Ecology and Culture of Water

With a natural groundcover of prairie or savanna, 40% of rainwater will evaporate, 30% will infiltrate deeply into the ground, 30% will infiltrate shallowly, and there will be no runoff.

With a 35% to 50% impervious surface, 25% of rainwater will evaporate, 20% will infiltrate deeply, 20% will infiltrate shallowly, and 35% will run off.

A clump of big bluestem penetrates deeply into the subsoil and carries some nutrients up and deposits them and hauls others down and stores them; the old passages of decayed roots open the soil to percolation and aeration; the brief cycle of an individual plant accelerates the process, while the thick surface network of rootlets (something that can hardly be washed or blown away) sponges up moisture and foods: in these ways the prairie builds soil from rock debris. As a whale surfaces for air, so big bluestem comes up for sunlight, but it too belongs mostly to a netherworld.

—William Least Heat-Moon, *PrairyErth*

With a 75% to 100% impervious surface, which is where our commercial areas are, and most of our residential areas with their sleek green lawns are, there is 15% evaporation, 5% deep infiltration, 5% shallow penetration, and 75% runoff. (NEMO Project Fact Sheet #3, Cooperative Extension Center, 1994.)

... our lives are diminished if we cannot establish rich and abiding contact with water.... Preserve natural pools and streams and allow them to run through the city; make paths for people to walk along them and footbridges to cross them.

... Whenever possible, collect rainwater in open gutters and allow it to flow above ground, along pedestrian paths and in front of houses. In places without natural running water, create fountains in the streets.

—Christopher Alexander, Sara Ishikawa,
and Murray Silverstein, *A Pattern Language*

AN ELEGANT SOLUTION: RAIN GARDENS

INSTEAD OF TREATING STORMWATER as waste and sending it through underground pipes, discharging it into creeks, rivers, detention ponds, and ultimately into the Gulf of Mexico, water can be used in a beautiful way. It runs through open, sinuous passageways that pour into pools, waterfalls, and fountains. Water flows down steps, cascades over walls, splashes among rocks, or sheets over ledges; it spouts high into the air or bubbles on the surface. It gushes; it surges; it trickles; it ripples; it is impossible to predict what water will do, other than flow downhill.

Water is easy to deal with in small amounts; it is when the aggregation becomes large that its force is overwhelming. When all the rainwater of a subdivision or town drains into a stormwater system, it becomes a problem; but if each house or building is dealt with individually, it is an opportunity to create beauty.

Catch the rain from your downspouts or water from your sump pump and direct it through a brick, paver, or stone-lined channel to a low area filled with wetland plants. If your house is situated on a hillside, you have the opportunity to create waterfalls and cascades that will flow and undulate down the slope and empty into a small pool.

Then arrange for all the rain that falls on your property to infiltrate the ground rather than be conveyed into a stormwater removal system. Here are some ideas:

➤ Create terraces and walks of smooth pavers with cracks between the stones for drainage. Fill the spaces with small, lime-loving plants to sponge up water and for their beauty (see "Terrace Tapestry").

➤ Build driveways out of crushed gravel edged with brick or make driveway ribbons similar to those built in the 20s and 30s. Construct them with paving stones or bricks and plant sun-loving, low-growing plants such as Wild Strawberry, Common Cinquefoil, Prairie Smoke, Prairie Phlox, Wild Petunia, Prairie Alum Root, Purple Love Grass, Scribner's Panic Grass, Buffalo Grass, and/or Path Rush between the ribbons. If you have a solid surface driveway, cut shallow channels horizontally across the width of the driveway so water drains into vegetated areas next to the drive instead of into the street and the stormwater system. Line the channels with brick or stone for a decorative effect

➤ Construct streets of brick pavers that absorb water through the cracks—more expensive to install than concrete or asphalt, but longer lasting, and therefore cost effective.

➤ Most important of all-fill your property with gardens of deep-rooted prairie and savanna forbs and grasses ❧.

A primary goal of sustainable design in building and site development should be, whenever possible, to retain water where it falls, treating the water as a resource, not discharging it as a waste product.

—James M. Patchett and Gerould S. Wilhelm,
The Ecology and Culture of Water

DESIGN FOR A TERRACE WITH RAIN CHANNELS

MY CLIENTS HAD ADDED a sunroom to their decidedly nontraditional country house. They wanted a new terrace built of the old brick rescued from a downtown street that had been torn up in the city we live in. They did not want gutters and downspouts—they wanted the rainwater to fall off the roofs into a pebble-lined shallow trench. I suggested, as an alternative, building rain channels under the drip line that would lead into small pools. The owners were enchanted and we built a ter-race with a paver-lined rain channel next to the sunroom that wound its way under a wooden bridge that led from the sunroom to an attached garden shed. The channel turned a corner, then ran next to the shed, spilling into a pool at the end of the channel. A spillway constructed of a double layer of flagstone crossed the terrace diagonally, a stunning counterpoint to the brick terrace. The terrace was edged with more flagstone that curved outward, echoing the curve of the garden next to it. ❧

Left: Before.

Right: After. Rain channel catches rainwater from roof along edge of new sunroom.

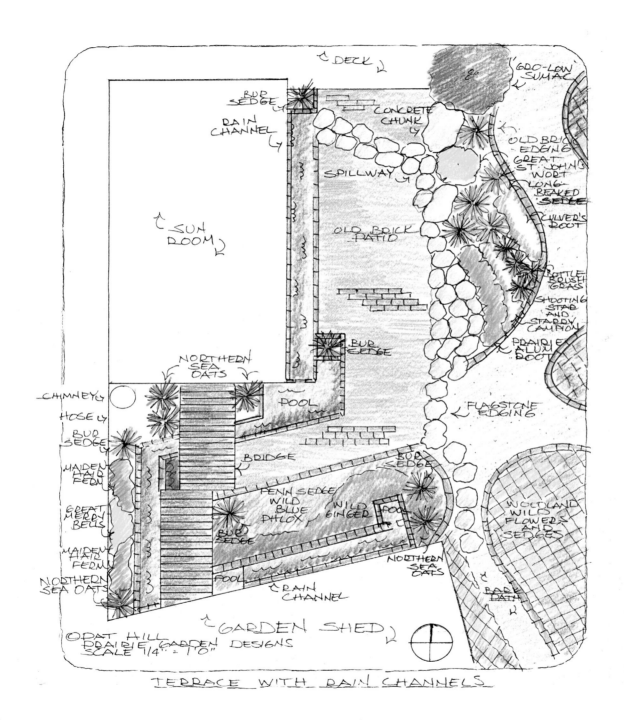

DECK

GRO-LOW SUMAC

BUR SEDGE

RAIN CHANNEL

CONCRETE CHUNK

OLD BRICK EDGING

GREAT ST. JOHN'S WORT

LONG BEAKED SEDGE

SPILLWAY

SUN ROOM

OLD BRICK PATIO

CULVER'S ROOT

BOTTLE BRUSH GRASS

SHOOTING STAR AND STARRY CAMPION

BUR SEDGE

NORTHERN SEA OATS

PRAIRIE ALUM ROOT

CHIMNEY

HOSE

POOL

FLAGSTONE EDGING

BUR SEDGE

BUR SEDGE

MAIDEN HAIR FERN

BRIDGE

PENN SEDGE WILD BLUE PHLOX

WILD GINGER

POOL

GREAT MERRY BELLS

WOODLAND WILD FLOWERS AND SEDGES

MAIDEN HAIR FERN

BUR SEDGE

NORTHERN SEA OATS

POOL

NORTHERN SEA OATS

RAIN CHANNEL

BACK PATH

GARDEN SHED

©PAT HILL PRAIRIE GARDEN DESIGNS
SCALE 1/4" = 1'0"

TERRACE WITH RAIN CHANNELS

Above left: Skilled workmen build rain channel and ...

Above right: ...bridge from sunroom to potting shed.

Below left: Rain channel and garden run next to potting shed with bridge in background.

Below right: Distinctive new terrace next to sunroom.

Swamp Milkweed
is a colorful addition
to wet or moist gardens,
in bloom in July
into August.

DESIGN FOR A DRAINAGE SWALE

THIS HOUSE HAD SEVERE WATER drainage problems. Situated on the side of a hill, the water that ran from the downspout on the south side of the house cut a channel through the lawn, eventually ending up in the common area savanna. The slope was gentle, and the problem was easily solved by planting a drift of water-absorbing Chokeberries (*Aronia arbutifolia*) at the mouth of the downspout that led into a vegetated swale planted with Swamp Milkweed, Spotted Joe Pye Weed, Marsh Blazing Star, Sneezeweed, Cup Plant, Blue Vervain, Ironweed, Ohio Goldenrod, Fowl Manna Grass, and Prairie Cord Grass. Intermittent, low, cobblestone dams slow down the water flow during heavy rains. Two other downspouts at the back of the house emptied into a bed of other moisture-loving plants that included Kalm St. John's Wort, Blue Vervain, Marsh Blazing Star, Mountain Mint, Winged Loosestrife, Northern Sea Oats, Long-beaked Sedge, and Wild Ginger. Clusters of small, white, flat buttons bloom on the leafy, multi-branched, 3′-tall Mountain Mint (*Pycanthemum virginianum*). The leaves are fragrant when crushed—use them to make an aromatic tea or to flavor lemonade. Mountain Mint blooms over a long season, from early July through August, in wet, mesic, and even dry prairies. It spreads quickly by underground stolons, especially in moist soil, so plant it with other strong growers.

The sloped area, next to the house, above the downspout, was, contrarily, a dry area, and the plants that were used reflect that situation. ∾

Drainage swale with tall yellow Cup Plant and rosy Swamp Milkweed and Spotted Joe Pye Weed.

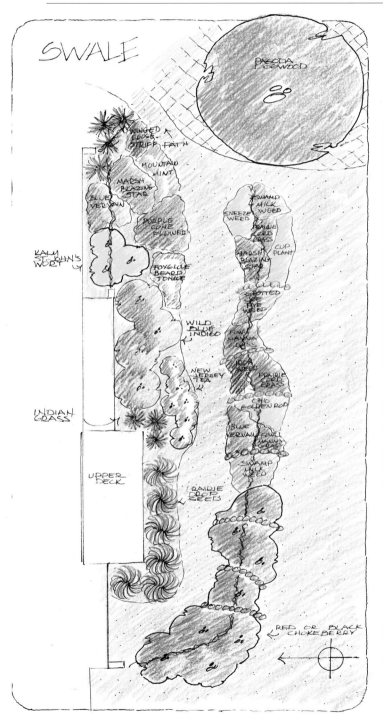

SWALE

PAGODA DOGWOOD

WINGED LOOSE STRIFF PATH

MOUNTAIN MINT

MARSH BLAZING STAR

BLUE VERVAIN

PURPLE CONE FLOWER

KALM ST JOHN'S WORT

FOXGLUE BEARD TONGUE

WILD BLUE INDIGO

NEW JERSEY TEA

INDIAN GRASS

UPPER DECK

PRAIRIE DROP SEEDS

SWAMP MILK WEED

SNEEZE WEED

PRAIRIE CORD GRASS

CUP PLANT

MARSH BLAZING STAR

SPOTTED JOE PYE WEED

FOWL MANNA GRASS

IRON WEED

PRAIRIE CORD GRASS

OHIO GOLDEN ROD

BLUE VERVAIN

FOWL MANNA GRASS

SWAMP MILK WEED

RED OR BLACK CHOKEBERRY

Marsh Blazing Star and Mountain Mint revel in water from downspout, while Purple Cone Flower thrives in drier sloped are further from the house.

DESIGN FOR A TERRACED HILLSIDE

THE PROBLEM ON THE NORTH side of the house was more serious. Five downspouts drained into a shady, narrow, steep slope between two houses; sheets of water washed down the hill and into the oak savanna during heavy rains. Grass didn't grow in that shady situation; the soil was wet and soggy in spring, hard-baked clay in the heat and drought of summer, and a sheet of ice in winter.

To solve the problem, flexible, "leaky" plastic drainpipes were attached to the ends of the downspouts and buried underground, thereby allowing the rainwater to drain out slowly along the way and eventually empty into a French drain at the bottom of the slope (a large hole in the ground filled with pea gravel). I then terraced the slope with a series of limestone walls, winding a flagstone path down the steps and around the corner leading to the brick patio. I planted lime-

stone-loving plants on both sides of the terraces, beginning with 'Annabelle' Smooth Hydrangea that grows in either sun or shade. On the shady side I planted Woodland Brome and ferns; while the sunniest part on the south side was filled with Prairie Smoke, Purple Prairie Clover, and Pale Purple Coneflower. In the partial sun/shade area in the middle around the path and steps, I planted New Jersey Tea, Wild Columbine, Wild Stonecrop, Thimbleweed, and Prairie Alum Root, along with Wild Petunia to cascade over the edge.

A distinctive Pagoda Dogwood grows at the bottom of the incline. The rest of the bed was filled with moisture-loving plants, such as Great St. John's Wort, Golden Alexanders, and Great Blue Lobelia. Tufted Hair Grass edges the stone path and the patio. What once was an unattractive, even dangerous slope became a delightful garden. ❧

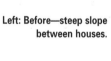
Left: Before—steep slope between houses.

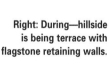
Right: During—hillside is being terrace with flagstone retaining walls.

TERRACED HILLSIDE

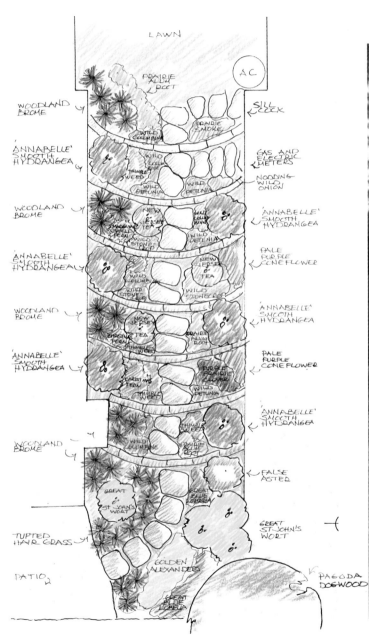

LAWN

AC

PRAIRIE ALUM ROOT

WOODLAND BROME

WILD COLUMBINE

PRAIRIE SMOKE

SILL COCK

'ANNABELLE' SMOOTH HYDRANGEA

WILD LUPINE

THIMBLEWEED

WILD PETUNIA

WILD PETUNIA

GAS AND ELECTRIC METERS

NODDING WILD ONION

WOODLAND BROME

NEW JERSEY TEA

WILD LUPINE

MARGINAL SHIELD FERN

WILD STONECROP

WILD PETUNIA

'ANNABELLE' SMOOTH HYDRANGEA

'ANNABELLE' SMOOTH HYDRANGEA

WILD COLUMBINE

WILD STONECROP

NEW JERSEY TEA

WILD STONECROP

PALE PURPLE CONEFLOWER

WOODLAND BROME

NEW JERSEY TEA

PRAIRIE ALUM ROOT

'ANNABELLE' SMOOTH HYDRANGEA

CHRISTMAS FERN

THIMBLEWEED

'ANNABELLE' SMOOTH HYDRANGEA

CHRISTMAS FERN

THIMBLEWEED

PURPLE PRAIRIE CLOVER

WILD PETUNIA

PALE PURPLE CONEFLOWER

THIMBLEWEED

'ANNABELLE' SMOOTH HYDRANGEA

WILD COLUMBINE

PRAIRIE ALUM ROOT

WOODLAND BROME

FALSE ASTER

GREAT ST JOHN'S WORT

GREAT BLUE LOBELIA

GREAT ST JOHN'S WORT

TUFTED HAIR GRASS

PATIO

GOLDEN ALEXANDERS

GREAT BLUE LOBELIA

PAGODA DOGWOOD

Finished terraced hillside. Golden Great St John's Wart blooms on the right; 'Annabelle' Hydrangea flourishes next to the terrace.

DESIGN FOR A RAIN GARDEN
Sun, Wet Soil

IF YOU HAVE A LOW SPOT on your property, don't fill it in with more soil—fill it in with plants that are indigenous to the moist prairie. Channel the rain from your roof or sump pump into this low area where the deep-rooted plants will absorb the excess moisture.

Golden Alexanders and Blue Flag bloom in May and June, while Marsh Phlox, Blue Vervain, Winged Loosestrife, and Narrow-leaved Loosestrife will start to bloom toward the end of June.

The sun-gold, umbellate blossoms of Golden Alexanders (*Zizia aurea*) are almost identical to those of Heart-leaved Meadow Parsnip, mentioned earlier. The leaves, however, are three-parted. It begins to bloom at the top of 1′ to 2′ stems in early May and continues into June—one might think Queen

Anne's Lace had turned to glowing gold. They prefer moist soils, but will also grow in dry upland savannas and prairies.

Fifty years ago, hundreds of Blue Flag (*Iris virginica var. shrevei*) lined the shores of the Fox River, says Dick Young in *Kane County Wild Plants & Natural Areas*—it must have been a spectacular sight! The graceful *fleurs-de-lis* of Blue Flag are azure blue; the white base of the down-curving sepals or falls is reticulated in blue and centered with a bright golden bee guide. (In some plants, the falls are entirely reticulated.) It grows 1′ to 3′ tall with stiff, sword-shaped leaves. In the wild it is found in marshy areas along the shorelines of streams, rivers, ponds, and lakes, and in fens; it will also grow in mesic garden situations. I planted a few near a downspout at my present house where they bloom beautifully. You may find Blue Flag listed in some wildflower books as *Iris versicolor*.

Rounded clusters of silken fuchsia flowers of Marsh Phlox (*Phlox glaberrima, var. interior*) begin to bloom at the top of 1′- to 3′-tall stems in mid- to late June. In moist or well-watered soils , as those fade, side shoots emerge and continue the flower show through August, with a few blossoms lingering into September. Marsh Phlox is found in swales within the prairie, in wet, calcareous meadows, and also in mesic situations. I grew it in ordinary soil in various places in my gardens, but it has always petered out after a few years.

The bright blue-purple flowers of Blue Vervain (*Verbena hastata*) form elegant candelabras at the top of 5′- to 6′-tall stems in July and August. Frequent in marshes and moist meadows, it, too, was a volunteer in my mesic garden. An aggressive seeder, it has created dozens of new plants; they tend

Blue flag and Golden Alexanders make a pretty combination in moist soils in June.

Golden Alexanders in
bloom near a pond.

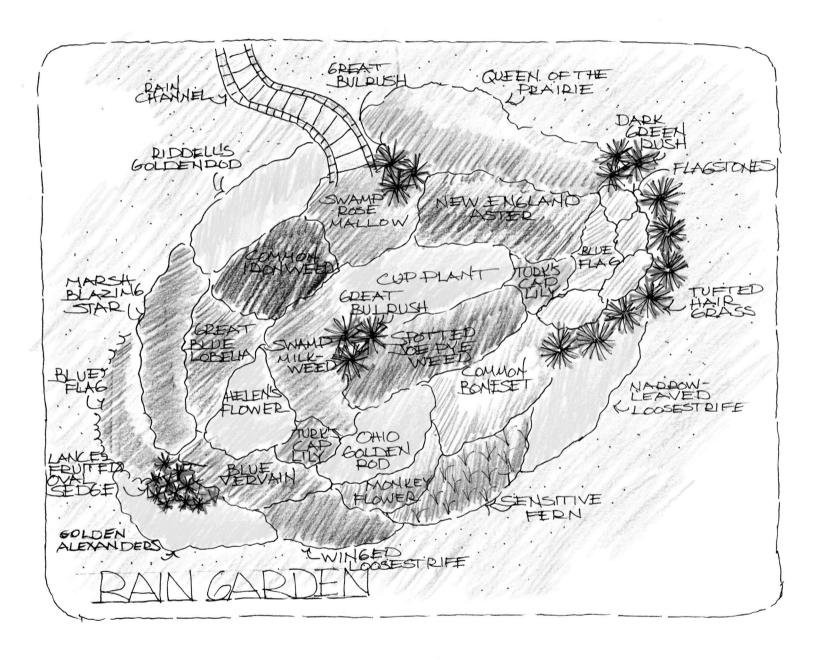

to die out, however, in seasons of drought.

Narrow-leaved Loosestrife (*Lysimachia quadriflora*) was a recent discovery for me. Four dainty, canary-yellow flowers bloom at the ends of sharply nodding stems; then the side shoots begin to bloom as well, each plant becoming a full bouquet. It blooms bountifully in July, with sporadic bloom into September. The stiff, narrow leaves grow in whorls around the stem. It's in perfect scale to the Winged Loosestrife (*Lythrum alatum*) in bloom at the same time. Dainty, cerise, tubular blossoms appear in the leaf axils up and down the branched stems all summer on a 1'- to 3'-tall, smooth, leafy plant.

Lysimachia translates into "loosestrife," but confusingly some members of the genus *Lythrum* are also called "loosestrife." The flowers of *Lysimachia* are golden, while those of *Lythrum* are pink or purple.

Most of the rest of the flowers will bloom in July and August. The brilliant, vivid, purple flower tufts of Common Ironweed (*Vernonia fasciculata*) grow in clusters in a flat corymb at the top of 2' to 4' red-purple stems. Its tough and fibrous stems give it its common name. It begins to bloom in mid-July and continues through August.

Dense, domed,delightfully fragrant calico clusters of deep rose and pale pink blossoms of Swamp Milkweed (*Asclepias incarnata*) bloom in July and August at the top of 2' to 4' smooth, branched stems. Its narrow, lance-shaped leaves distinguish it from other milkweeds. It's found in wet prairies, marshes, fens, swales, and along the shores of ponds, streams, and rivers. (I planted three plants in mesic soil near a downspout at my house, but they only survived a couple of seasons.)

Spotted Joe Pye Weed (*Eupatorium maculatum*) is a magnificent flower, 5' to 6' tall, topped with flat cymes of showy,

Above: The Golden Cup Plants and purple Common Iron Weed contrast dramatically in moist soils in July.

Below: Spotted Joe Pye Weed thrives next to creek.

Common Boneset, Spotted Joe Pye Weed, and Cup Plant prosper in wet alkaline wetland in Bluff Spring Fen in Elgin, Illinois.

rose-plum blossoms deliciously fragrant with the scent of vanilla. A cousin of the Purple Joe Pye Weed, its flowers are flat rather than domed, are a deeper pink, and its stems are spotted. Its July to September blossoms are wildly attractive to butterflies and bumblebees.

The fuzzy, bright-white, flat-topped flower clusters of Common Boneset (*Eupatorium perfoliatum*) bloom at the top of 4′ plants in August and September. Its stems appear to "perforate" the clasping leaves, as suggested by the plant's scientific name. It thrives in marshes, fens and bogs.

Fragrant, feathery plumes, the color of crushed raspberries, bloom at the top of 4′- to 8′-tall stems of Queen-of-the-Prairie (*Filipendula rubra*) in July. One of our most spectacular wildflowers, its huge, toothed palmate leaves give it a tropical look. Somewhat aggressive, it spreads by rhizomes, soon forming large clumps.

Tiny, individual, gleaming-golden blossoms form a flat-topped cluster at the top of the 2′ to 3′ stems of Ohio Goldenrod (*Solidago ohioensis*). It's a long-blooming plant, which can start to flower as early as mid-June and not quit until the end of October. Found in fine marshes and fens, it makes a colorful tapestry with New England Aster and Spotted Joe Pye Weed.

New England Aster (discussed earlier) and Riddell's Goldenrod wait until September and October. The flowers of Riddell's Goldenrod (*Solidago riddellii*) are bunched in a dome-shaped arrangement at the ends of corymbose branchlets on 1′- to 3′-tall stems. Its unique, vertically folded, arching leaves are an easy identification mark. It blooms from early September through October in wet prairies and marshes; it also thrives in mesic gardens. (Two of these plants appeared spontaneously in the third year of my prairie garden and are doing well.)

The flat-topped, canary-yellow Ohio Goldenrod flourishes near Fox River.

The sedges, grasses, bulrushes, and ferns provide refreshing green all season.

page 179

DESIGN FOR THE SHORELINE OF A SMALL POND

Sun, Wet Soil

THIS IS A SMALL INFORMAL pool edged with flagstones, cobbles, and pebbles, planted with emergents and pond's-edge plants. The sedges begin to bloom in May, followed by Blue Flag in June. Most of the rest of the flowers will bloom in July and August.

Many of the plants grow in the shallow water near the edge of the pond. Delicate, white umbel flowers that resemble Queen Anne's Lace bloom at the top of the 6′ stems of Tall Water Parsnip (*Sium suave*) from mid-July to mid-September. Frequent in marshes, it is also found in ditches and in shallow ponds where Buttonbush is a common companion. Buttonbush (Cephalanthus occidentalis) is a loosely branched, rounded shrub 3′ to 6′ tall, with lustrous bright green leaves in summer. The "buttons" are delightful creamy, stamen-covered 1″

balls on long stalks that appear in July and August. It is found in sunny marshes or shaded floodplains.

The blue-purple, two-lipped blossoms of the Monkey Flower (*Mimulus ringens*) somewhat resemble a monkey's face; therefore the genus and common name. The vertical upper lip is two-lobed; the three-lobed lower lip has two yellow spots to guide bees to the throat and stamens. Long-blooming, it flowers from late June through August. Its square, 1′ to 3′ stems are clad with opposite, lance-shaped, sessile leaves. It is found in marshes and along the muddy shores of rivers, streams, and pond edges, and in ditches. A few seeds of Monkey Flower hitchhiked their way, via a pot of Culver's Root, into my mesic garden where they germinated and bloomed delightfully. The plants didn't appear, however, in 2002, an especially hot, dry summer.

Left: The umbel flowers of Tall Water Parsnip somewhat resemble those of Queen Anne's Lace.

Right: The distinctive, stamen-covered, ball-shaped flowers of Buttonbush make the shrub easy to identify.

In the shallow water the flowers of pickerel weed were lavender shadows.
At the water's edge Mittie found a stalk of white three-petaled flowers in whorls of three.
—Elizabeth Lawrence, ***Through the Garden Gate***

The gorgeous Pickerel Weed flourishes in a pond at the Chicago Botanic Garden.

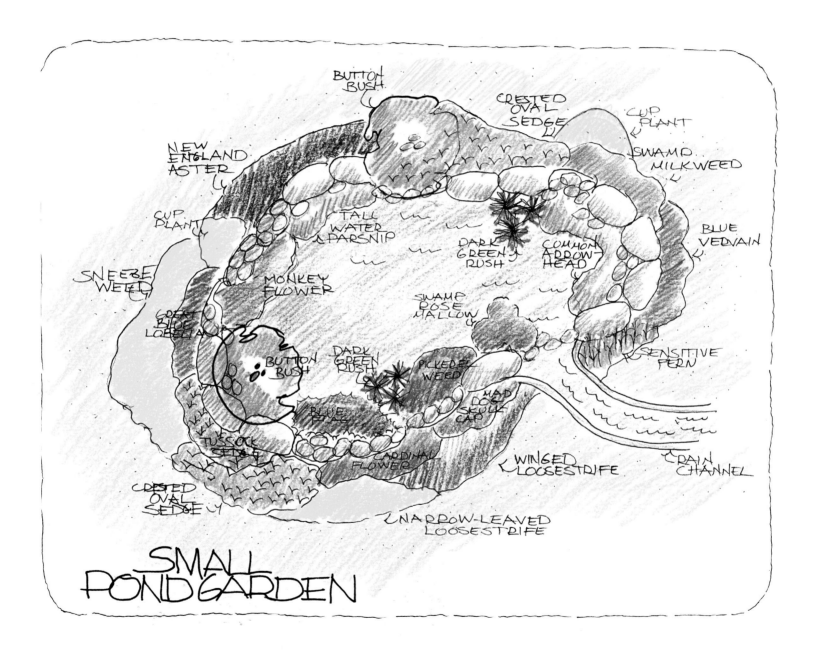

SMALL POND GARDEN

The dazzling sapphire-blue spike flowers of the Pickerel Weed (*Pontederia cordata*) bloom above elongated heart-shaped leaves from late June through mid-September. It is found in the still water along the edges of ponds and lakes or slow-moving streams. Its submerged roots are also a tasty treat for muskrats.

Distinctive, dark-green arrowhead leaves identify Common Arrowhead (*Sagittaria latifolia*). Bright-white, golden-centered, three-petaled flowers bloom in whorls of three around a tall, stiff stalk during July and August. The underwater rhizomes produce starchy tubers that are relished by ducks and muskrats. Indians also availed themselves of this nutritious foodstuff-they not only gathered the roots at the source but also opened muskrat houses to take the cache of roots stored there (William Niering and Nancy Olmstead, *The Audubon Society Field Guide to North American Wildflowers, Eastern Region*). ✎

Above: The blue-violet candelabras of Blue Vervain are prolific seeders in wet or moist soil.

Below: Queen-of-the-Prairie is one of the most spectacular Midwestern native plants.

CONCLUSION

*The Indians knew that life was equated with the earth and
its resources, that America was a paradise, and they could not
comprehend why the intruders from the East were determined to
destroy all that was Indian as well as America itself.*

—Dee Brown, *Bury My Heart at Wounded Knee*

HOW TO PLANT A PRAIRIE GARDEN

SO HOW DOES ONE GO about planting a Prairie Garden? Not like one might think.

Choose an open sunny site that gets full sun for at least six hours a day.

First remove the sod. The quickest method is with a sod cutter—you can rent one yourself or hire someone to do it for you. (The sod that is removed can be fashioned into a mound or small berm—green side down—but wait a season for the grass to die before planting.) Other ways to kill the sod are with Roundup or by smothering it with black plastic or newspapers topped with leaves, mulch, or sand. But unlike how we have always been taught to plant gardens, do not till the soil! Disturbing the soil brings up weed seeds to the surface—we want to avoid that.

Then cover the entire area with a layer of finely shredded hardwood mulch. Choose prairie plants growing in $2^1/2''$ pots (I used mostly $2^1/2''$ pots in my first garden along with a few gallon containers—the plants from the $2^1/2''$ pots caught up with the gallon container plants by the end of the 1st season). Then lay out the plants in their pots, 1' on center, in a design you find pleasing. Plant each species in drifts, dense at the center, feathering out at the edges, intermixing with the species next to it, so the edges are blurred. When you are satisfied with their arrangement, you can plant them. Remove the plant from its pot by turning the pot upside-down and slightly squeezing it. If it is root bound—the pot is completely filled with roots_take a knife and score all four sides of the root ball before planting. This will encourage the plant to make new

Page 184: The magnificent leaves and tall stems of Prairie Dock accent this long prairie border Wild Quinine, Purple Coneflower, and Yellow Coneflower are in bloom in July

Left: Foxglove Beardtongue blooms in June in the prairie garden along with Butterfly Weed and Pale Purple Coneflower.

roots where it has been cut. (If you don't cut the roots, it could be months before it sends out new roots into the surrounding soil; it will need constant watering until it does so.) Then brush aside the mulch where you want to install your plant, dig a hole the same size as the root ball, then put the plant in the hole—do not plant it lower than the grade. Firm the soil around the plant and replace the mulch. Continue until all the plants are installed. When you're done, water each plant individually and thoroughly. (I've never used mulch for my own prairie gardens and have had very few problems with weeds. But it does present a neater appearance, so I do it for clients.)

That's it! You will need to do some supplementary watering in the heat of summer the first year or two; but after that the roots will be deep enough to draw water up from the sub-

soil. There might be some weed seeds that blow in and will take root on top of the mulch; you'll have to remove those. In the second and third year, self-sown prairie forbs and grasses will appear, softening and blurring edges even more. Usually the new seedlings will be close to the plants they have fallen from, but many times they will appear at a distance—embrace serendipity.

Don't deadhead, don't fertilize, and don't spray with anything—no pesticides, herbicides or fungicides. You will, in all probability, get some mildew and some bugs in the first few years; I did, but my garden is so lush and bountiful that little imperfections are not noticeable. Aphids and milkweed bugs attacked my Butterfly Weed at first, but they no longer do. In native landscaping and gardening the plants do the work for us.

One garden won't save the world—but a subdivision of native plants will do some good. ❧

The art of living is the accomplishment and the fulfillment of our task during our sojourn on this earth. Those who observe the rules of life are a part of the endless chain of evolution and are happier human beings than those who have drifted into a self-centered life of excess, of arrogance and conceit, destroying themselves and leading others on false trails.

—Jens Jensen, *Siftings*

Ackerman, Diane. *A Natural History of the Senses.* New York: Random House, 1990

Alexander, Christopher, Sara Ishikawa, Murray Silverstein. *A Pattern Language.* New York: Oxford University Press, 1977

Antonio, Thomas M. and Susanne Masi. *The Sunflower Family in the Upper Midwest.* Indianapolis: The Indiana Academy of Science, 2001

Boon, Bill and Harlen Groc. *Nature's Heartland.* Ames, Iowa: Iowa State University Press, 1990

Chicago Historical Society. "Prairie in the City: Naturalism in Chicago's Parks, 1870-1940," edited by Rosemary Adams. Chicago: Chicago Historical Society, 1991

Dirr, Michael A. *Manual of Woody Landscape Plants,* 4th Edition. Champaign, Illinois: Stipes Publishing Company, 1990

Dickenson, Emily. *Favorite Poems of Emily Dickenson.* Edited by Mabel Loomis Todd and T.W. Higginson. New York: Avenel Books, 1978

Duchscherer, Paul and Douglas Keister. Outside the Bungalow, America's Arts and Crafts Garden. New York: Penguin Studio, 1999

Greenly, John. *The Encyclopedia of Ornamental Grasses.* Emmaus, Pennsylvania: Rodale Press, 1992

Grese, Robert E. *Jens Jensen.* Baltimore: The Johns Hopkins University Press, 1992

Eisenberg, Evan. *The Ecology of Eden.* New York: Alfred A. Knopf, 1998

Jenson, Jens. *Siftings.* Baltimore: The Johns Hopkins University Press, Paperbacks edition, 1990

Kirt, Russell R. *Prairie Plants of the Midwest: Identification and Ecology.* Champaign, Illinois: Stipes Publishing L.L.C., 1995

Kornwolf, James D. "The Arts and Crafts in American Houses and Gardens""an essay in *The Ideal Home,* 1900-1920.New York: Harry N. Abrams, Inc., 1993

Lacey, Stephen. *The Startling Jungle.* Boston: David R. Godine, Publisher, 1990

Ladd, Doug. *Tallgrass Prairie Wildflowers.* Helena, Montana: Falcon Press, 1995

Lawrence, Elizabeth. *Through the Garden Gate.* Edited by Bill Neal. Chapel Hill, N.C.: The University of North Carolina Press, 1990

Least Heat-Moon, William. *PrairyErth*. Boston: Houghton Mifflin, 1991

Legler, Dixie and Christian Koreb. *Prairie Style Houses and Gardens by Frank Lloyd Wright and the Prairie School.* New York: Stewart, Tabori & Chang

Leopold, Aldo. *A Sand County Almanac.* New York: Oxford University Press 1968

Madson, John. *Where the Sky Began: Land of the Tallgrass Prairie.* Ames, Iowa: Iowa State University, 1982

Marinelli, Janet. *Stalking the Wild Amaranth.* New York: Henry Holt and Company,. 1998

Mattoon, W.E. and R.B. Miller. *Forest Trees of Illinois*, 1927. Revised by Dr. George D. Fuller. Springfield: Department of Conservation, Division of Forestry, State of Illinois, 1955

Mikula, Rick. *Garden Butterflies of North America.* Minocqua, Wisconsin: Willow Creek Press,1997

Miller, Wilhelm. "The Prairie Spirit in Landscape Gardening" Urbana, Illinois: University of Illinois College of Agriculture, 1915

Newcomb, Lawrence. *Newcomb's Wildflower Guide.* Boston. Little, Brown and Company, 1977

Oehme, Wolfgang and James van Sweden, with Susan Rademacher Frey. *Bold Romantic Gardens.* Herndon, Virginia. Acropolis Books, Ltd., 1990

Packard, Stephen and Cornelia F. Mutel, editors. *The Tallgrass Restoration Handbook.* Washington, D.C. :Island Press, 1997

Pollan, Michael. *Second Nature: A Gardener's Education.* New York: The Atlantic Monthly Press, 1991

_____*A Place of My Own.* New York: Random House, 1997

Poor, Janet, editor. *Plants That Merit Attention, Volume I –Trees.* Portland, Oregon: Timber Press, 1984

Runkel, Sylvan T. and Dean M. Roosa. *Wildflowers of the Tallgrass Prairie: The Upper Midwest.* Ames, Iowa: Iowa State University Press, 1989

Sackville West, Vita. *The Illustrated Garden Book.* Anthology by Robin Lane Fox. New York: Atheneum, 1989

Sperka, Marie. *Growing Wildflowers: A Gardener's Guide.* New York: Harper & Row, 1973

Shirley, Shirley. *Restoring the Tallgrass Prairie.* University of Iowa Press: Iowa City, 1994

Still, Steven M. *Manual of Herbaceous Ornamental Plants*, 4th Edition. Champaign, Illinois: Stipes Publishing Company, 1994

Sullivan, Jerry. *Chicago Wilderness: An Atlas of Biodiversity.* Chicago. Chicago Region Biodiversity Council. (no date given)

Swink, Floyd and Gerould Wilhelm. *Plants of the Chicago Region*, 4th Edition. Indianapolis: Indiana Academy of Science, 1994

Thom, James Alexander. *Follow the River.* New York: Ballantine Books, 1981

Walton, Richard K. *National Audubon Society Pocket Guide: Familiar Butterflies of North America.* New York: Alfred Knopf, 1990

Wilder, Louise Beebe. *Color In My Garden.* New York: Atlantic Monthly Press, 1990

Wilson, Helen van Pelt and Leonie Bell. *The Fragrant Year.* New York: M. Barrows & Company, Inc, 1967

Young, Dick. *Kane County Wild Plants & Natural Areas.* Geneva, Illinois: Kane County Forest Preserve District, 1994

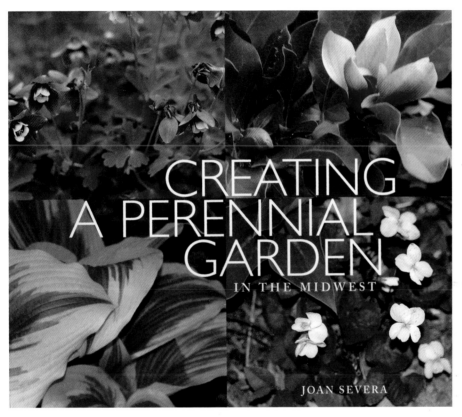

CREATING A PERENNIAL GARDEN IN THE MIDWEST

Joan Severa

Combining wisdom and warmth, master gardener Joan Severa helps you create
beautiful gardens with healthy perennials ideally suited for zones 3, 4 and 5.
Emphasizing basic techniques, she demystifies and simplifies Midwest gardening
with a common sense approach every gardener will appreciate. Stunning full-color
photos inspire you to create your own garden sanctuary.

Softcover | 10 x 9 | 184 pages | List $29.95
ISBN: 0-915024-73-X

MIDWEST COTTAGE GARDENING
Frances Manos

Create your own beautiful cottage garden! This practical book will help Midwestern gardeners—whether novices or old pros—achieve beautiful, organic gardens drawing on age-old cottage garden traditions. Learn how to plan and plant a bountiful garden with a lively mixture of perennials, annuals, fruiting trees and shrubs, vegetables and herbs.

Softcover | 10 x 9 | 184 pages | List $29.95
ISBN: 1-931599-40-8

**For these and other great Trails Books titles, call (800) 258-5830
or visit us online at www.trailsbooks.com**